Peter Linstead is a barrister specialising in Employment Law, with a commercial focus. He has over 20 years' experience of acting in High Court employment disputes. He is a member of Outer Temple Chambers and was formerly the Head of the Employment Group in another leading common law chambers in London. He is frequently instructed in High Court claims relating to the termination of employment, in particular interim injunction applications and claims for damages based on breach of fidelity and fiduciary duties. He also acts in claims relating to bonus schemes and long-term incentive schemes and has extensive experience in High Court claims for workplace stress and harassment.

Peter is ranked as a "leading junior" in UK Employment Law by Legal 500 and acted in some of the most important recent cases concerning both disability discrimination and employment status in the 'gig economy'. He has appeared without a leader in the Court of Appeal on a range of matters including public sector equal pay and race discrimination. He writes and lectures extensively on Employment Law. He is the Editor of the Tolley's Employment Law Service section on '*Absence from Work*'. He is an active member of the Education and Training Committee of the Employment Lawyers' Association.

Peter also has an international practice focussing on the Courts of the DIFC in Dubai and he is instructed in a range of cases in that jurisdiction, including injunction applications. He has expertise in the DIFC's Court Rules and Employment Law and was recently instructed by the DIFC Authority to advise on aspects of the drafting of their primary legislation. He also advises in the Isle of Man jurisdiction.

Restraining Competition by Employees

A Practical Guide to Restrictive Covenants, Injunctions and Other Remedies

Restraining Competition by Employees

A Practical Guide to Restrictive Covenants, Injunctions and Other Remedies

Peter Linstead
Barrister, Gray's Inn
MA (Hons)(Oxon)

Law Brief Publishing

Published 2020 by Law Brief Publishing, an imprint of Law Brief Publishing Ltd
30 The Parks
Minehead
Somerset
TA24 8BT

www.lawbriefpublishing.com

Paperback: 978-1-912687-38-1

For Emily

PREFACE

My aim is to create the book which I wish had been available when I first started appearing in the High Court as a (very) junior barrister, instructed at short notice to defend a number of interim injunction applications, invariably where employers were seeking to stop departing employees from dealing with their clients. A further aim is to demystify an area which tends to be seen as highly specialist, within the wider employment law community.

There are already some excellent books which cover the legal practice and procedure relating to employee competition, comprehensively and at length. By contrast, this book is intended to provide both an indexed 'quick reference' guide and an explanation of the things which matter most when making decisions about current or intended litigation in this area, particularly in relation to injunctions, restrictive covenants and damages relating to competitive activity. It is deliberately short, so as to assist the reader to understand quickly how a given area works, with a focus on the most recent developments. It is nevertheless written in enough detail to be of real assistance to legal practitioners.

For his invaluable research skills and editing assistance, I would like to thank Matthew Shore.

I am also extremely grateful to Keith Bryant QC for his comments on an earlier draft of this book.

The law is stated as the author understands it to be as at 30th June 2020.

Peter Linstead
London
June 2020

TABLE OF CASES

TABLE OF LEGISLATION

CONTENTS

CHAPTER ONE
INTRODUCTION

1.1.   <u>The purpose of this book</u>

1.1.1. Employers want their employees to remain loyal and want to stop them from

- removing and using confidential information about their clients and business processes,

- taking their customers, and

- competing.

1.1.2. Preventing a former employee from using his or her skills and knowledge to make a living, even if those skills have been taught by the former employer, is an unlawful restraint of trade. The law permits interference with the employee's freedom in this area only to the very limited extent necessary to protect an employer's legitimate interest. Nevertheless, the law will provide a remedy if the employee has committed or threatens to commit an unlawful act (usually a breach of contract or a breach of confidence).

1.1.3. The purpose of this book is to explain, in a concise and understandable format, the ways in which the law provides a remedy in this situation. It is also a step-by-step guide to the relevant procedure. The intention is to focus on the most common issues that arise in these cases, the main forms of remedy and the most important recent cases rather than to provide an exhaustive catalogue of this area of law, which can be found in other publications.

1.1.4. It is aimed not only at solicitors, general counsel and barristers who seek a better understanding of this area and who may need to take a client's claim through the courts, but also at human resources professionals and those on both sides in the workplace who are facing a dispute involving alleged competition by the (ex)employee. It has been assumed that the reader has a basic familiarity with legal concepts and at least some experience of employment law. The layout of this book should enable the reader quickly to gain an understanding of the steps most commonly taken in the legal process where there has been actual or alleged competitive activity and the legal framework within which that sits. These topics are approached both from the perspective of employers and employees. However, it is acknowledged that many of the chapter headings are written from an employer's perspective. This is because a key aspect of understanding how the law works in this area lies in analysing the various remedies available to employers and how they would get the matter into court.

1.1.5. It is intended to approach this subject from a practical perspective in two ways: first, by providing practical suggestions and a road map to those advising employers and employees where the employee is suspected of competitive activity or removal of confidential information, including guidance as to the procedure to be followed when injunctions and other forms of relief are sought in court; secondly, where case law is used to explain how the law works in particular areas, the aim is to assist the reader's understanding as to how arguments might be put on behalf of the employer or employee rather than to explain the historical development of the law or to summarise every relevant case.

1.2.   The scheme of this book

1.2.1. Following the Introduction, Chapter 2 looks at some of the relevant considerations whilst the employment relationship is still subsisting, including recent cases on introducing new post-termination restrictions ("PTRs").

1.2.2. Chapters 3 to 8 are short chapters which take the reader through the steps in the legal process from the point at which there is suspected wrongful activity by an employee through to an injunction application and interim hearing, focussing on the practical things that matter along the way. Injunctions are only one of many aspects of the law of employee competition. But faced with the question of how to prevent competitive activity, if the lawyers have not been able to resolve matters through pre-action correspondence, an injunction application is the most likely way in which the employer will try to use the legal process to restrain that activity. The matters covered in these chapters include the use of undertakings; considerations relevant to whether to apply for an injunction; the practicalities of lodging an application including paperwork, issue fees and the relevant sections of the Civil Procedure Rules; without notice applications; ways of obtaining disclosure and evidence including computer imaging and inspection, search orders and delivery up; the court's approach to an injunction application; the orders and directions likely to be made; and things that can go wrong in interim applications.

1.2.3. The final four chapters, which are longer and are subdivided into headings, cover more of the substantive law in this area, whilst maintaining a practical approach.

1.2.4. Chapter 9 considers confidential information: how is it defined and how can it be protected? This chapter includes the significant impact on this area of the Trade Secrets (Enforcement, etc.) Regulations 2018. Recent cases looking at the impact of the Human Rights Act 1998 on confidential information injunctions are also considered.

1.2.5. Chapter 10 considers the question of what to do if there are no contractual restraints on soliciting and competing. This covers areas of law and causes of action which apply independently of any express PTRs in the employment contract. It covers the differences between the contractual duty of fidelity and fiduciary obligations, preparations for competition, springboard injunctions, garden leave injunctions and the Copyright and Rights in Databases Regulations 1997.

1.2.6. Chapter 11 is devoted to express restrictive covenants, their interpretation and enforcement. This includes understanding how the courts will interpret them and the considerations applying to how they should be drafted and whether or not they will be upheld. Whilst a variety of covenants is considered, the main focus is on non-solicitation, non-dealing and non-competition clauses, which are in practice the most significant express restraints, and the ones giving rise to the most controversy. This chapter also considers in detail the recent Supreme Court decision in *Egon Zehnder Ltd v Tillman* [2020] AC 154 which is of fundamental importance to the issues of severance and to the construction of covenants generally.

1.2.7. Chapter 12 covers damages and in particular negotiation damages following the Supreme Court decision in *Morris-Garner v One Step (Support) Ltd* [2018] 2 WLR 1353, claims for wasted management time and claims for repayment of salary.

1.2.8. Given the deliberate aim of keeping this book concise and practical, some areas which are relevant to employee competition cases are covered in summary form because a detailed examination of the relevant law would be voluminous. Nevertheless, an effort has been made to present the essential points in each of these areas. These include the economic torts, the Copyright and Rights in Databases Regulations 1997, Human Rights Act defences to confidential information injunctions, confidential information clauses and non-poaching clauses. For the same reason, the court's approach to assessing common law and equitable damages in employee competition cases is covered only in overview, but there is detailed consideration of 'negotiation' or 'Wrotham Park' damages and some other creative forms of damages claims.

1.2.9. The threat of adverse costs orders also has enormous tactical significance in this area. The civil costs regime is a specialist subject in its own right and this book does not cover the general costs provisions of the Civil Procedure Rules 1998. There is however detailed reference to some specific costs considerations and to indemnity costs in particular.

1.2.10. A further topic which could have filled several chapters is how to go about gathering evidence of wrongdoing by an employee, both before and after the termination of employment. Whilst acknowledging that in certain industries, this is a question of real practical importance, there is not space here for a full treatment of this issue. But the topic is covered in overview and the reader will certainly get a sense of the extent of evidence which the court would require from many of the cases which are summarised below. There is also a thorough examination of the powers of court to order one of the parties to provide information, disclosure, or delivery up and to make an order for the examination of computers, which is becoming an increasingly important part of employee competition cases.

1.2.11. This book covers the law of England and Wales. Whilst many of the principles considered are applicable in Scotland, it is acknowledged that there are some differences between the English and Scottish systems in relation to contract law, statute law and procedure. An analysis of these differences has not been undertaken, in the interests of brevity.

CHAPTER TWO
ISSUES DURING
EMPLOYMENT

Disciplinary procedures, garden leave, introducing new restrictive
covenants and settlement agreements

2.1   <u>Discovering preparatory or competitive activity whilst the</u>
       <u>employee is still employed</u>

2.1.1 Frequently, competitive activity is only discovered after an
       employee has departed. If, however, the employer is fortunate
       enough to discover it whilst the employment relationship is
       ongoing, there are a number of measures which can be taken.

2.1.2 All employees are subject to an implied contractual duty of
       fidelity. There is a significant volume of case law on the point at
       which acts by an employee in preparation for competitive
       activity will breach this duty – certainly not all preparatory acts
       will do so – and the problem of identifying this point is con-
       sidered in detail in later chapters. Nevertheless, if it can be
       established that an employee's activities breach this implied
       term, it is likely that the breach is a repudiatory breach of con-
       tract and potentially gross misconduct, which can provide a
       basis to bring disciplinary proceedings.

2.1.3 A decision will need to be taken whether to suspend the
       employee during any investigation. This may be necessary to
       allow an investigation to proceed without hindrance. However,
       suspension also has certain disadvantages, in that it will be very
       difficult to control and monitor the activities of the employee.
       Indeed, if they are already secretly contacting the employer's
       clients, it may give them a greater opportunity to do so.

2.1.4　During an investigation, one of the obvious places to look for evidence of wrongdoing is the employer's computer systems and, to the extent it is possible to do so, electronic devices held by the employee. The following considerations are relevant to this search.

i　It may be necessary at an early stage to appoint an independent IT expert to assist with this process.

ii　It is important to be clear about the extent to which the employer has the right to monitor and search the employee's work email and instant messaging. Monitoring of employees at work involves the processing of personal data and, as such, is regulated by the GDPR. Consequently, various safeguards are needed such as considering and documenting the legal grounds for processing personal data in the context of monitoring. Consent will not likely be valid in an employment context, but the employer's legitimate business interests might be relied on instead as a legitimate basis to access the information. Of course, the whole process will be more straightforward if the employer has written monitoring policies in place, for all employees, in advance of these activities being carried out.

iii　Instant messaging and 'chat room' histories can be very revealing and are increasingly being used as a source of evidence in proceedings. Whilst disclosure of an employee's personal chat history could only be obtained via court proceedings, there are often work-based instant messaging platforms, such as Bloomberg and Skype Instant Messenger for Business, which can legitimately be accessed from the employer's systems.

iv　Customer relationship management systems with contact details may show in their histories when information was accessed by the relevant person and whether it has been downloaded to other computers or storage devices.

v Unusual requests for downloads or prints of information such as customer contact information may be revealing.

vi Social networking sites such as Facebook, LinkedIn and Twitter can provide a surprising amount of information about employees' activities. Given the ability of employees to upload and remove information quickly, it is prudent to take screenshots of material which is discovered in this way.

2.1.5 If the employer decides to run disciplinary proceedings, it is particularly important to take care that any process is run fairly. A failure to do so might amount to a repudiatory breach of contract by the employer, either of the terms of a contractual procedure or of the implied term of trust and confidence. The employee might then resign and claim constructive dismissal, and in this instance, the employee would allege that any restrictive covenants in the employment contract are not enforceable because of the employer's breach. Alternatively, if the employer terminates the contract following an inadequate procedure, the employee could still contend that the employer has committed a repudiatory breach and consequently that s/he is not bound by restrictive covenants.

2.1.6 If the employee's actions suggest that s/he will leave imminently to join a competitor, the employer might wish to invoke garden leave provisions in the contract, under which the employee would be bound by the duty of fidelity throughout the notice period. This avenue could be used whether or not there are also PTRs. The use of garden leave injunctions to force the employee to comply with the contract in these circumstances is considered in detail in chapter 10 below.

2.2 Introducing new restrictive covenants

2.2.1 It is common for employers, during the currency of employment, to seek to get employees to enter into restrictive covenants which were not originally contained in their contracts.

2.2.2   Clearly the first step would be to get the employee to agree to new restrictions. If he or she will not agree and it is an absolute imperative for the business to secure the protection of restrictive covenants, the extreme solution is dismissal, coupled with an offer of immediate re-engagement on the revised terms. This is a risky course which should not be embarked upon without legal advice. Hopefully the employee will agree, making this course unnecessary.

2.2.3   However, in addition to securing agreement, it is well established that an employer who wishes to get an employee to enter into new and/or more onerous restrictions needs to provide the employee with separate valuable consideration. It is not enough for the employee merely to sign the new contract. Where an employer seeks to impose substantial new obligations on an existing employee, the consideration must comprise 'some real monetary or other benefit (promotion for example) conferred on the employee for the purpose of causing the employee to agree the restrictive covenant' and it must be 'substantial and not nominal'.[1]

2.2.4   Matters commonly relied upon as consideration in these circumstances are pay rises, promotion, training and continued employment in circumstances where the employer can satisfy the court that had the employee not agreed, the employment would have been terminated.

2.2.5   This principle was applied by the High Court in *Re-Use Collections v Sendall* [2015] IRLR 226 and it resulted in a senior employee not being bound by restrictive covenants in a new contract which he had signed. The defendant was a senior

---

1   This is the agreed statement of principle which was adopted by the Judge in *Re-Use Collections v Sendall* [2015] IRLR 226

employee of a glass recycling business. He had formerly owned it as a family business. Shortly before his departure, the claimant had given him a new contract of employment including restrictive covenants, which he signed. Around the time he signed the new contract, he had received an increase in salary. The Judge found there was no consideration for these new covenants. The claimant said that the consideration was (i) his increase in salary; and (ii) his continued employment. The Judge found there was no evidence that either was directly referable to the covenants, as the employer had not made it clear that either was linked to, or conditional upon, the defendant's entry into the restrictive covenants. There was no evidence that had he not entered the covenants, his employment would have come to an end. In the absence of express restrictive covenants, the employer's case could only be based on the implied duty of fidelity. This aspect of the case is considered in more detail below.

2.2.6   Two other recent cases have applied the same principle but in each case it was found that separate valid consideration had been provided.

2.2.7   In *Pickwell v Pro Cam CP Ltd* [2016] EWHC 1304 (QB) the claimants were trainee agronomists, learning to advise farmers on the purchase and use of agricultural chemicals, who had received a written offer of employment and had signed a document accepting that offer. Some weeks later, they signed a contract of employment containing the disputed restrictive covenants. After training with the defendant by shadowing other agronomists and then working independently advising farmers for a short period, they were then offered employment by a different company and brought a claim disputing the validity and enforceability of the covenants. Judge Curran QC found that the relevant legal principles were as follows:

(1) The burden was on the defendant to establish that the claimants were bound by the contracts containing the restrictive covenants.

(2) If express consent to the contracts could not be established, the case would turn on the issue of implied or inferred consent.

(3) To establish such consent it is for the employer to show an "unequivocal act implying acceptance" per Jacobs LJ in *Khatri v Cooperatiev Centrale Raiffeisen-Boerenleenbank BA* [2010] EWCA Civ 397, [2010] IRLR 715.

(4) In that regard, the EAT decision in *Solectron v Roper* [2004] IRLR 4 (approved in *Khatri*) was important, in particular per Elias P at para 30: "*is the employee's conduct, by continuing to work, only referable to his having accepted the new terms imposed by the employer?*"

(5) The intention of the parties and the fact of acceptance or otherwise is, in accordance with the ordinary principles of contract, to be objectively ascertained.

(6) Even in the situation of an alteration to the advantage of the employee, the 'only referable' test had to be satisfied: *Khatri*.

(7) Where a person alleges inferred or implied acceptance, he must show that the benefit invoked was only available pursuant to the contract in question, and that the invocation of that contractual right was in unequivocal terms, such as to be referable only to acceptance of that contract: *FW Farnsworth v Lacy* [2012] EWHC 2830, [2013] IRLR 198.

2.2.8 On the facts, the contract had been determinable on only one week's notice during the probationary period. The evidence was that their employment would have been terminated if they had refused to sign the amended terms. There was no evidence that they had objected to its terms at the time of signature. The case could be analysed as either the formation of a completely new contract or as a variation of the existing terms of contract concluded by the acceptance of the offer letters. The claimants' conduct in continuing to work under the contract was only referable to their having accepted the new terms, which included the restrictive covenants. There was, therefore, sufficient consent. The defendant had also conferred benefits upon the acceptance of the formal contracts which amounted to valuable consideration, by providing them with status and training in the field.

2.2.9   In *Decorus v Penfold* [2016] EWHC 142 (QB), the High Court applied the same principles. The claimant had been subject to a 9-month non-competition clause. In May 2013 he signed a new contract with more extensive PTRs lasting six months. The Court had to decide which applied. Whilst the claimant had received a pay rise, that had happened a few weeks before he signed. The Court accepted the employer's evidence that had he not signed the new contract, he would have been dismissed. It held that taken together the employee's appraisal, a pay rise and continued employment were valid consideration in the particular circumstances, because the appraisal and pay rise were part of a three-phase process, in which the signing of the new contract was the final phase.

2.2.10 As can be seen from the cases above, the High Court has made different decisions on facts which appear at first sight to be quite similar. However, the cases are fact sensitive and everything turns on whether the acts relied on to constitute consideration are genuinely referable to the change in contractual terms to the detriment of the employee.

2.3   Tactics when the employee leaves – termination agreements

2.3.1   There might be a need for a settlement agreement, for example, if the parties are in dispute, if there is a redundancy situation or if the departing employee was also a shareholder, such that a share purchase agreement is necessary on departure. Even if the restrictions in the employment contract were adequate, there is obvious value in the employee making a further express commitment to be bound by them and agreeing in writing that they are reasonable. This is given added force by the fact that the employee cannot validly enter into the agreement without the benefit of legal advice. Whilst an agreement that the clauses are reasonable would not prevent the court subsequently assessing their validity under restraint of trade principles, it would nevertheless be of some evidential value.

2.3.2   From the employee's perspective, a discussion of restrictive covenants at the point of leaving may give them the opportunity to try to agree any variation which will assist them in the next stage of their career. Alternatively, they may try to agree a list of restricted clients, in order to avoid any ambiguity about who might be approached.

2.3.3   Where there are no, or inadequate, restrictions in the contract of employment, an employer might wish to introduce specific time-limited restrictive covenants in a settlement agreement. If new restrictions are being entered into via a settlement agreement, that will be a new contract or a variation of an existing one and it is therefore important that consideration is given. This would need to be specified as separate consideration by, for example, a proportion of any payment made under the agreement being allocated specifically to consideration for the new restrictive covenant.

2.3.4   Settlement agreements generally include a prohibition on the use of the employer's confidential information after termination. Whilst confidential information is protected by equitable duties after the employment has terminated, it is valuable to have an express clause to make clear what information is protected, particularly if there are specific business processes and information which the employer seeks to protect. The settlement agreement will also include provision for the employee to return any confidential information and/or irrevocably delete it from his or her computer and phone and to return electronic devices belonging to the employer. The importance of the court upholding confidentiality provisions properly entered into as part of a settlement, where there has been legal advice and no pressure to enter into the agreement, has recently been re-stated by the Court of Appeal in *ABC v Telegraph Media Group Ltd* [2019] EMLR 5.

2.3.5   It is worth emphasising that the employer cannot, by reference to any contract term, seek to exclude the operation of the whistleblowing provisions of the Employment Rights Act 1996 ("ERA") (see s.43J ERA). This is a limit to the employer's ability to prevent the divulging of confidential information via a settlement agreement.

CHAPTER THREE
WHAT TO DO AFTER THE EMPLOYEE HAS LEFT

Gathering evidence, the purpose of undertakings and dealing with threats to compete

3.1 The initial steps and seeking undertakings

3.1.1 There are often suspicions but it is frequently unclear what exactly the employee is doing after departure. It is important for the employer to act swiftly, as soon as suspicions arise, as any injunction application should be made as soon as possible. Whilst it might be hard to find out what the ex-employee is now doing, in the majority of cases where confidential information (e.g. customer lists) is removed, it is stored electronically. There is often a trail which IT experts can discover by examining the employee's email, phone and/or computer. Unless it is one of the exceptional cases where it is felt better not to warn the employee that their ex-employer is aware of their activities, the next step is correspondence.

3.1.2 Initially, communication via a solicitor's letter is often the most effective way to warn an employee and potentially to set up a claim. If it appears the employee has taken confidential information, such as customer lists, the employer should ask for it back. If the employee is breaching the terms of restrictive covenants in the contract, the employer should demand that they desist. If the nature of their activities is unclear, a letter could be written asking what they are doing. If the employee fails to engage or gives evasive answers, that may be helpful evidence in a future claim.

3.1.3 In all these cases, it can be helpful to ask for undertakings, both for tactical reasons and because it is hoped that the employee will agree to abide by them. The form of undertaking may follow the wording of a restrictive covenant and restrain specified activity for the duration of the existing PTR. However, there are circumstances where a different period, or an open-ended period, could be relied on. For example, an undertaking might be sought where there are no PTRs and an employee is alleged to have taken confidential information during employment.

3.2 Status of a voluntary undertaking

3.2.1 The employer's solicitor often demands written undertakings as a condition of not proceeding to court. This will be a written undertaking that the (ex)employee shall not engage in certain behaviour and could include, for example, an undertaking to abide by restrictive covenants. Such undertakings will have the status of a contract: consideration is provided by the forbearance to sue. The employer could rely on a subsequent breach as a basis for injunction proceedings. Breach could be relied on as evidence of untrustworthiness or bad faith and may also help the employer in relation to costs arguments.

3.2.2 Arguably, an employee's acceptance of undertakings demonstrates a degree of acceptance that restrictive covenants are reasonable and/or enforceable. If it is not intended they should have that effect, from the employee's perspective it is best to include a carve-out to the effect that they are entered into without admission as to the reasonableness or enforceability of covenants.

3.2.3 If undertakings are not given before the court, any cross-undertaking in damages which they include is potentially unenforceable. For this reason potential defendants who are willing to give undertakings sometimes allow the claimant to proceed with an application to court purely for the purposes of obtaining a cross undertaking in damages. This could be dealt with by a consent order.

3.2.4 There are various tactical considerations. There are sometimes disputes between employer and employee as to what the correct scope of the undertakings should be. From the employer's perspective, care should be taken not to seek undertakings which are wider than is really needed, as it may be necessary subsequently to justify the position to a court.

3.2.5 On the other hand, employees should consider offering undertakings in open correspondence rather than without prejudice. This could then be relied on in court in relation to whether an injunction should be granted and to questions of costs. As the following case demonstrates, an interim injunction might be refused where the offer of an undertaking is a "sensible and proportionate" response to the application.

3.2.6 In *Whitfield & Brown (Development) Ltd v Osborne* [2014] EWHC 3908 (QB) a quantity surveyor ("QS") had a PTR stopping him carrying out any work which competed with business which he personally had been materially involved with whilst working for the claimant ex-employer. He went to work for another company, B, shortly after termination. The claimant claimed he had mentioned the name of a potential client at interview with B, and both the claimant and B were competing for the same contract. The claimant sought an injunction preventing him working as a QS for B. B and the surveyor, who were joint defendants, offered an undertaking that he would not be working on any contracts that the claimant was also competing for. That was refused and the claimant proceeded with the application for an injunction.

3.2.7 The Court held that mentioning the name of a potential client at interview was not a breach of the duty of fidelity, whereas providing details of the claimant's bid for that client might have been. By the time of the injunction application, the particular contract had already been offered to B and an injunction was refused. If the claimant had accepted the undertaking which B and the surveyor had offered, the surveyor would not be competing with any business carried on by the claimant. The undertaking was a sensible and proportionate response.

3.2.8   It is important to understand the degree to which an employer might rely on the refusal to give undertakings, or to give the correct undertakings, as a basis for saying that an employee is likely to breach covenants in the future. This argument is frequently made by employers but it would be unwise to bring an injunction application relying only on this point. As the following case demonstrates, an employee may legitimately refuse to give undertakings where they are unnecessary and there has been no actual unlawful behaviour.

3.2.9   In *Niit Technologies v Sudhir Chaturvedi* (High Court QB 10.3.17), a senior employee in a technology company had PTRs preventing solicitation of customers and enticing away other employees. He left and went to work immediately for another company in the information technology sector. Two months later one of his former direct reports also went to work there. The company asserted in correspondence that the employee's move was connected to the defendant and therefore a breach of covenant, which he vehemently denied. They wrote again asking for an undertaking that he would abide by the restrictive covenants. He refused as there was no basis on which an undertaking could reasonably be requested. There was no evidence of customers being solicited or of them mysteriously deserting and his connection to the other employee could not be inferred. The Court rejected the argument that the only reasonable inference it could make from the refusal to give an undertaking was that the defendant intended to break the covenants. There was no evidence to support the contention that there was a serious issue to be tried and the injunction was refused.

3.3   Undertakings given to court

3.3.1   Often once an injunction application has been made, a holding position can be reached pending a further return date, or pending trial, by the defendant giving undertakings to the court. This is done in practice by passing a consent order to the court with the form of undertakings included in the body of the order. The following points should be noted:

    i   For an (ex-)employee defendant, this is preferable to the court ordering an injunction as it gives control over wording of the order and (possibly) costs paid to the claimant.

    ii   The whole matter might be settled on the basis of court undertakings, particularly where they have a time limit matching the length of a restrictive covenant; a consent order would then stay proceedings, save for the purpose of enforcing the undertakings.

    iii   The undertaking is given to the court and not to the other side. As a result, breach is a contempt of court, which could result in prison, a fine or seizure of assets.

    iv   The undertakings should include a cross-undertaking in damages. In fact, a cross-undertaking in damages will be implied where an undertaking is given to the High Court (Chancery Guide para 16.29) but nevertheless, it is usual practice and sensible to make this an express term of the order. This is usually in the following form:

> *"If the Court later finds that this Order has caused loss to the Defendant, and decides that the Defendant should be compensated for that loss, the Claimant will comply with any order that the court may make."*

3.3.2   Real care should be given to the duration of any undertaking. The order may say "until trial or further order" but the representatives of employees should be careful to ensure there is a long stop date, to allow for the fact that the case might settle and there may never be such a trial.

3.4   Getting out of undertakings / acceptance of the validity of covenants

3.4.1   In *Capgemini India Private Ltd (and ano'r) v Krishnan* [2014] EWHC 1092 (QB) the Court considered the position where undertakings had been given but then withdrawn by the defendants. This included the question of whether the undertakings indicated that they accepted the covenants were valid. A group of employees serviced only one particular client and had restrictive covenants preventing them for six months after termination from dealing with any customer with whom they had business dealings in the last six months of their employment. The company lost the account and a competitor signed a five-year contract with the client. The employees resigned and worked their notice, then began working for the competitor on the same account. The company said they would apply for an injunction in the absence of written undertakings prohibiting them from working on the account. The employees gave the undertakings, on legal advice, in order to avoid the cost of proceedings, but then withdrew them on learning that their employer would meet any costs of legal proceedings. The company applied for an injunction contending that the giving of undertakings debarred the employees from challenging the reach and effect of the restraint of trade clause and that damages were not an adequate remedy.

3.4.2   The Judge refused to grant an injunction pending trial. Whilst agreements were to be encouraged on public policy grounds, the fact the undertakings were given was not an unassailable bar preventing the defendants from making submissions in relation to the validity of the restraint of trade clause. The real issue was whether the company had established a basis to find that an injunction was necessary and just to protect a legal right. They had lost the account, had no prospect of regaining it and damages would be an adequate remedy. The injunction was refused.

3.5   Responding to the threat of an injunction on behalf of an employee

3.5.1   If it is clear that your employee client has

   i   breached restrictive covenants which are arguably enforceable, and/or

   ii   removed confidential information whilst still working for his/her previous employer, and/or

   iii   otherwise breached express or implied terms of the contract whilst still employed,

it may be worth offering, or agreeing to give, undertakings at an early stage. Employers frequently demand payment of their legal costs where undertakings are offered late, after the commencement of a legal process.

3.5.2   Whilst there may be circumstances in which the employee should push back (see above), if your instructions are that s/he has no intention of wrongdoing, there may be little to lose by giving undertakings pre-action.

CHAPTER FOUR
THE DECISION WHETHER OR NOT
TO GO FOR AN INJUNCTION

When is there sufficient evidence and do you need to show financial loss?

4.1.   <u>The decision to go for an injunction or not</u>

4.1.1. Employers often know of or suspect competitive activity. The perennial question is at what point is there enough to convince a court that an injunction is needed.

4.1.2. The threshold question at interim injunction stage is whether there is a 'serious question to be tried'. Unless the material fails to disclose that the claimant has any real prospect of succeeding, the court should go on to consider the balance of convenience (*American Cyanamid* [1975] AC 396, pp407B and 408G). The serious question to be tried is a "minimalist" threshold "which sets [the test] at a level which does little more than exclude claims which might be characterised as frivolous or vexatious" (*Bartholomews v Thornton* [2016] IRLR 432 para 10).

4.1.3. Whilst it may be "minimalist" there still needs to be some evidence of unlawful activity, either before the employment terminated or subsequently.

4.1.4. It is also important to note that an injunction is potentially available to restrain unlawful conduct, actual <u>or threatened</u>. If the conduct has not yet taken place it is known as a *quia timet* ('because he fears') injunction. In order to justify a *quia timet* injunction there must be a "cloud which was clearly visible on the horizon": *Papamichael v Nat West Bank plc (No 1)* [2002] All ER (Comm) 60, para 61.

4.1.5. It follows that an employee who contends in correspondence that his/her restrictive covenants are unenforceable (either because of the way they are drafted or because of a repudiatory breach by the employer) and that they therefore intend to engage in competitive activity, is in a difficult position. This is because the employer may rely on that statement as a basis to seek an injunction to restrain threatened competition and because generally arguments about enforceability are left for trial and will not prevent an interim injunction. The only way in which an employee can be sure of his/her position is to issue proceedings to obtain a declaration as to the enforceability of restrictions, but that is an extreme and potentially costly option.

4.1.6. It is unlikely that a court would be persuaded to treat a mere assertion that covenants were unenforceable, without more, as a threat that the employee will engage in behaviour contrary to those covenants (see *RSM Tenon Ltd v Cocking* [2013] EWHC 846 (QB), where the Judge described correspondence of this nature as "shadow boxing"). However, employee representatives should be extremely careful of crossing the line and indicating that the employee may or will engage in competitive activity, notwithstanding the covenants, because of the use which may be made of this assertion by the (ex-)employer.

4.2. <u>Evidence of approaching customers</u>

4.2.1. For the purposes of an application for an injunction, if what is being relied upon is breach of a non-solicitation clause or approaching customers in breach of a duty of fidelity, some actual evidence of contact with customers is generally necessary. The wording of any relevant covenant ("solicitation"/ "supply services to" etc.) affects the evidence required. Anecdotally, a very small number of examples will suffice, if they evidence a clear breach of a restrictive covenant which the employee must have (or ought to have) known about. The position is more difficult when what is relied on is an inference that an employee has misbehaved. In that case, the court will require as much relevant evidence to be presented as possible. A mere suspicion will clearly not be enough to persuade a court that there is a 'serious issue to be tried'.

4.2.2. It can assist to put the allegations as precisely as possible to the (ex-)employee in correspondence. Failure to contest allegations is often relied on in support of an injunction. However, unless there is a specific admission, it would be unwise for an employer to rely purely on the employee's answers to correspondence, even if they are evasive. The relevance of the manner in which the employee engages with correspondence about undertakings is considered in detail above.

4.3. Delay

4.3.1. Delay may count against the award of an injunction. It is one of the factors feeding into the judge's consideration of whether it is 'just and convenient' to grant the injunction. A long and unexplained delay is likely to be fatal. However, ultimately it is not the length of the delay that matters but the reasons for it and its effect on the utility of an injunction. The best way to illustrate this is through the use of two examples from the case law.

4.3.2. Delay might be relied on as evidence the employer does not need the interim injunction. It could also mean that the employee has taken on commitments (for example starting a new job) which it would be unjust to prevent him from fulfilling.

Where delay is fatal

4.3.3. In *Legends Live v Harrison* [2016] EWHC 1938 (QB) Edis J set out the two-stage approach for determining whether an injunction should be refused on the ground of delay: first, the delay must be unreasonable; and secondly, it must be unjust in all the circumstances to grant the relief sought.

4.3.4. In *Legends Live* the claimant operated a tribute show in Blackpool, for which the defendant had worked as a performer. The defendant left the claimant to perform for a rival show on Central Pier in breach of his non-competition covenant. The claimant's solicitors set a deadline for him to agree to comply with his express restrictive covenant and not perform, which was two days before the first performance. The defendant declined to agree but no proceedings were instituted until two months later after he had been performing for two months.

4.3.5. Edis J found that had the application for an injunction been made before the first performance, it would have been granted. That would have given time for the rival show to prepare its season without the defendant. However, were the application now before him to be granted, considerable disruption would be caused to the Central Pier and to the rival show. He noted that the position of third parties may be a relevant factor when determining whether it is unjust in all the circumstances to grant the relief sought. Consequently, it did not matter that neither the Central Pier nor the rival show were parties to the proceedings.

4.3.6. In the absence of any explanation for the delay, the judge could only conclude that the claimant was seeking to cause avoidable loss and destruction to a rival. It was not the length of the delay which mattered but the reason and the circumstances.

Where delay is not fatal

4.3.7. In *Baker Tilly UK Holdings v Clough* [2013] EWHC 3616 (QB), the defendants were accountants and senior employees of the claimants. The defendants' contracts of employment contained PTRs not to solicit certain clients and not to solicit certain employees. The defendants resigned within a 6-day period of each other in May 2013. Each defendant had to give six months' notice and they were placed on gardening leave. The claimants sought deeds of undertaking, by which the defendants agreed to be bound by their covenants. Due to changes in the structure of the employer's business, which involved a TUPE transfer, the defendants' employment came to an end on 28 September 2013. The claimants wrote to the defendants seeking confirmation by 30 September that they intended to abide by their covenants. The defendants' solicitors wrote back denying that the covenants were binding and raising various arguments as to why this was the case. On 2 October, the claimants became aware that the defendants were working for a competitor. The claimants wrote again to the defendants' solicitors, providing detailed responses to their assertion that the covenants were not binding and giving a deadline of 7 October for assurance that the defendants would comply with their PTRs. When that assurance was not forthcoming, the claimants issued an application for interim injunctive relief on 11 October, returnable on 17 October, when the application was heard. Due to the short time available to the defendants before the hearing, it was agreed that the substantive claim would be heard on 24 and 25 October. Full trial of the issues would not take place until February 2014. The claimants sought an injunction to last for the short period before the hearing on 24 October: a period of about one week.

4.3.8. The defendants submitted that the claimants had no real need of this injunction because they had been aware that the defendants did not consider themselves bound by the covenants and had been working for the competitor since 2 October. They had let this situation go on for two weeks without seeking relief: they did not now need immediate relief for the short period before the next hearing. Swift J held that the claimants had not delayed in bringing proceedings. They had made genuine attempts to put their case to the defendants and address their arguments. This was a reasonable and responsible course to adopt and one that should be encouraged. Further, the delay of one week could well be very damaging to the claimants.

4.4. <u>Is it necessary to establish that there will be damages at trial in order to get an injunction?</u>

4.4.1. It is not necessary, for the purposes of obtaining an interim injunction, to show that if the matter proceeds further the claimant will have a quantifiable, or indeed any, claim for damages available to it.

4.4.2. In *D v P* [2016] IRLR 355 the Court of Appeal said that absence of damage to the claimant is not in general a bar to relief save where there is exceptional prejudice or hardship to a defendant; and the starting point in the consideration of a claim by an employer to enforce an employee's negative covenant is an injunction.

4.4.3. The position was explained in more detail in *Insurance Co v Lloyd's Syndicate* [1995] 1 Lloyd's Rep 272 at 277 where Colman J stated:

> "*The effect of the authorities can be summarised as follows:*
>
> *1. Express or implied negative covenants will in general be enforced by injunction without proof of damage by the plaintiff.*
>
> *2. The principle does not depend on whether the plaintiff is a person or a corporation. The ready availability of the remedy is not the consequence of equity's regard for the plaintiff's personal feelings but of equity's perception that it is unconscionable for the defendant to ignore his bargain.*
>
> *3. Although absence of damage to the plaintiff is not in general a bar to relief, there may be exceptional cases where the granting of an injunction would be so prejudicial to a defendant and cause him such hardship that it would be unconscionable for the plaintiff to be given injunctive relief if*

he could not prove damage. In such cases an injunction will be refused and the plaintiff will be awarded nominal damages."

4.4.4. In *Dyson v Pellerey* [2016] ICR 688, Sir Colin Rimer approved the foregoing, save that he did not regard the word "exceptional" as appropriate, saying that the categories of circumstances in which the court might refuse an injunction were not closed.

CHAPTER FIVE
HOW TO LODGE THE APPLICATION IN COURT AND THE INTERLOCUTORY HEARING PROCESS

How to lodge the application in court and the interlocutory hearing process

5.0.1. A decision has to be made as to which court the application is going to be issued in. Interim relief in an employment context can be sought in the Queen's Bench Division or the Chancery Division of the High Court. Injunctions can, in most cases, also be sought in the County Court although it is more common for injunctions in employee competition cases to be sought in the High Court. There is no monetary limit on the jurisdiction of the County Court to award damages in actions in contract and tort. Circuit Judges can grant injunctions but they have limited powers to grant search orders and freezing injunctions.

5.0.2. The following proceedings would have to be brought in the Chancery Division, as opposed to the Queen's Bench Division or County Court, as a result of Schedule 1 to the Senior Courts Act 1981 ("SCA") which gives the Chancery Division exclusive jurisdiction in "patents, trade marks, registered designs, copyright or design right":

    i. claims based on the Copyright and Rights in Databases Regulations 1997;

    ii. claims otherwise involving copyright or intellectual property.

5.0.3. In other cases, there is a free choice and the issue fees are the same in the County Court and High Court. Proceedings "for damages or for a specified sum" must be issued in the County Court unless the value is more than £100,000 and the High Court will scrutinise carefully whether money claims under £500,000 should be in the County Court. However, a claim which includes a claim for an injunction falls under SCA s.37 which gives the power to grant an injunction to the High Court. The High Court will therefore not transfer a claim which includes an injunction application to the County Court.

5.0.4. Practical considerations will include the degree of urgency required. In the writer's experience, the hearing for an on-notice injunction will be listed more quickly in either division of the High Court than in the County Court. The High Court also deals with far more injunction applications than the County Court so the outcome is likely to be somewhat more predictable. The procedures for obtaining an interlocutory hearing in the Chancery Division are different from those in the Queen's Bench Division, as will be explained below.

5.1. <u>The rules</u>

5.1.1. The court's power comes from SCA S37: the High Court may grant an injunction in all cases in which it appears to the court to be just and convenient to do so. The County Courts Act 1984 s.38 provides that generally the County Court may make any order which could be made by the High Court if the proceedings were in the High Court.

5.1.2. By CPR rule 25.1

(1) The court may grant the following interim remedies –

(a) an interim injunction(GL);

(b) an interim declaration;...

By rule 25.2

(1) An order for an interim remedy may be made at any time, including –

(a) before proceedings are started; and

(b) after judgment has been given.

(Rule 7.2 provides that proceedings are started when the court issues a claim form.)

(2) However –

(a) paragraph (1) is subject to any rule, practice direction or other enactment which provides otherwise;

(b) the court may grant an interim remedy before a claim has been made only if –

(i) the matter is urgent; or

(ii) it is otherwise desirable to do so in the interests of justice;

…

(3) Where it grants an interim remedy before a claim has been commenced, the court should give directions requiring a claim to be commenced.

5.2.   When is it appropriate to apply without notice?

5.2.1. In *Moat House Group South Ltd v Harris* [2006] QB 606, it was held that "to grant an interim remedy in the form of an injunction without notice is to grant an exceptional remedy" and further that "the more intrusive the order, the stronger must be the reasons for the departure from the usual rule that applications should be heard inter partes" (see para 63).

5.2.2. By CPR rule 25.3

> *(1) The court may grant an interim remedy on an application made without notice if it appears to the court that there are good reasons for not giving notice.*
>
> *(2) An application for an interim remedy must be supported by evidence, unless the court orders otherwise.*
>
> *(3) If the applicant makes an application without giving notice, the evidence in support of the application must state the reasons why notice has not been given.*

5.2.3. In addition PD 23A sets out (at para 3) circumstances in which an application can be made without notice, which include "where there is exceptional urgency". More detail on the considerations which determine this question can be found in the Queen's Bench ("QB") Guide (sections 13 and 14) and Chancery Guide (paras 16.2-16.6) at Volume 2 of the White Book.

5.2.4. The court should not entertain an application of which no notice has been given unless either giving notice would enable the defendant to take steps to defeat the purpose of the application or there has been literally no time to give notice before the remedy is required: *National Commercial Bank Jamaica Ltd v Olint Corp Ltd (Practice Notice)* [2009] 1 WLR 1405 (PC).

5.2.5. An attempt should be made to give at least informal notice by telephone, although that might be excused where the notice itself might defeat the interests of justice. It has been said that the widespread use of mobile devices for sending and receiving information makes it unlikely there will ever be a practical reason why an applicant should not give at least informal notice to a respondent (see for example *Jeeg Global v Hare* [2012] EWHC 773 (QB)).

5.2.6. In the context of employee competition, *CEF Holdings Ltd v Mundey* [2012] IRLR 912 (QB) provides guidance as to when a without notice application should be heard. In that case, the applicants submitted that the need for an injunction enforcing post-employment restraints was a matter of exceptional urgency. The Judge (Silber J) disagreed and said that an application for such an exceptional remedy will need to be carefully justified by more than a "bland statement that the defendant might do something if warned". Further, "[a]ny application for an injunction must be based on facts and … mere suspicion is not enough". The Judge considered the relevant factors in determining the question of urgency: (1) what damage is likely to have accrued to the applicant between the date of the without notice application and the proper return date if proper notice had been given? (2) How long had the applicant known about their possible claims and how did they react? The Judge also noted that "the restrictions sought to be imposed were onerous because of the restrictive covenants and the springboard relief" and so the burden on the applicants was higher.

5.2.7. In that case, the Judge found that the applicants were not entitled to make their application without notice. Amongst other things, they had not acted as if the matter was one of exceptional urgency when they had first discovered the alleged wrongdoing. Concern about future staff defections and the refusal of some respondents to give undertakings or reply to correspondence were not enough to justify the without notice application.

5.2.8. Silber J therefore discharged injunctions which had been made earlier by a judge on half a day's notice to the defendants, so effectively *ex parte*, stating that 3 days was the minimum period specified to allow the defendant to be fully and properly prepared. On the return date, he also refused to order continuing injunctions on various grounds, including the fact that the restrictive covenants relied on were not enforceable.

5.2.9. It should be noted that in cases of extreme urgency, an application can be made outside court hours, and there is a duty judge for that purpose.

Duty of full and frank disclosure

5.2.10. More generally, *CEF Holdings* highlights some of the other hurdles which will be faced on a without notice application. The Judge also considered the evidence that would be required to comply with the heightened duty of disclosure, which should include a witness statement setting out the duty to give full and frank disclosure and then indicating how the duty has been complied with. That duty was not altered in the present case just because the defendants had attended the initial hearing with counsel and on half a day's notice.

5.2.11. Further guidance on the nature of the duty was provided in *Wild Brain Family International v (1) Robson & (2) Chubb* [2018] EWHC 3163 (Ch). In this case, the claimant successfully obtained injunctive relief (delivery up, evidence preservation and computer imaging) following a without notice application. The defendant made an application to discharge the order, partly because the grounds for making a without notice application had not been made out. The Judge disagreed, holding that there was a real possibility documents would have been destroyed if it had been made on notice.

5.2.12. The defendant also contended that the duty of full and frank disclosure had not been complied with. The Judge rejected this argument and dismissed the discharge application. The duty on the applicant is to make "a full and fair disclosure of all the material facts". Before making the application, the applicant must make proper inquiries. The proper extent of these inquiries depends on all the circumstances of the case including: (1) the nature of the case; (2) the order sought and its likely consequences for the defendant; (3) the degree of urgency and time available for the inquiries. Departure from the basic principle that the court will hear both sides before making its decision means that the applicant must present evidence in a fair and even-handed manner, drawing attention to evidence and arguments it can reasonably anticipate the absent party would want to make. The key touchstone is whether the presentation of the application is fair.

5.2.13. The duty rests upon both the applicant's legal advisors and the applicant himself/herself. The legal team must ensure their client is aware of the duty and what it means in practice. This is important because often the applicant will be the only one with knowledge of all the material facts.

5.2.14. In *Wild Brain*, the applicant was held to have discharged its duty. Some of the key factors in that decision were as follows.

(i) The fact that non-disclosure is innocent, in the sense that the relevance of the material fact is not perceived, is an important factor but not decisive, by reason of the duty to make proper enquiries.

(ii) In respect of the respondents' contention that the applicant should have made more of the proposition that "orders for the early provision of information or early disclosure of documents are exceptional," the applicant had satisfied its duty of full and frank disclosure by drawing the Court's attention to the relevant passage in the relevant employment law textbook in its skeleton argument. Incorrect submissions or arguments will not amount to non-disclosure provided they do not deprive the Court of knowledge of any material circumstance. The applicant is not required to take the Court to cases which the respondent might wish to have drawn the Court's attention to in the same way as the respondent would have done so long as the applicant has fairly drawn the Court's attention to the principles derived from those cases.

(iii) The respondents contended that the applicant should have pointed out that the respondents might have argued, if present at the hearing, that it was not necessary to make the delivery up order at that hearing. However, in its skeleton argument, the applicant had made the point that the respondents would be likely to argue that the order was not so urgent as to justify being made without notice. Further, an intervention by the Judge had indicated that he clearly had in mind the question of whether it was necessary to make the order. The applicant had therefore complied with its obligation.

(iv) The Judge was well aware that compliance with the injunction sought would be onerous and the applicant did not need to do anything further to draw the Judge's attention to this issue. The applicant had made it sufficiently clear to the Judge how invasive the order would be.

(v) The applicant was not under a duty to draw the Judge's attention to the fact that by complying with the delivery up order, the respondents might have to deliver up material confidential to third parties: at the time the order was made, the applicant did not know, nor ought it to have known, that the respondents would in compliance with the order deliver up information confidential to third parties.

(vi) As part of its case, the applicant alleged that the respondents had wrongfully diverted the opportunity to acquire a certain YouTube channel away from the applicant. The respondents argued that the applicant had not properly addressed in its evidence the likelihood that it might not have been able to acquire the channel. However, the applicant had said to the Judge that the respondents were likely to argue that it didn't have sufficient funds to acquire the channel and in light of the fact that the respondents' ability to pay was still an issue in dispute in the case, in all the circumstances the applicant had discharged its duty.

Claims where enforcing restrictive covenants is not sought

5.2.15. A distinction can be drawn between without notice applications for injunctive relief that enforce PTRs and without notice applications for delivery up orders or search orders. With regard to the latter, it is of course often likely that notice will enable the defendant to defeat the purpose of the application.

5.2.16. This distinction is illustrated by *Hyperama Plc v Poulis* [2018] EWHC 3483 (QB). In this case the claimant made a without notice application for an order prohibiting the use or disclosure of confidential information by the defendants, an order enforcing restrictive covenants in the defendants' employment contracts and a doorstep delivery up order (which is defined below).

5.2.17. The application for the doorstep delivery up order could be granted because had notice of the application been given, it would have enabled the defendants to defeat the purpose of the relief sought. However, the Court emphasized that the application in this case should be limited to only those issues where notice would defeat the purposes of injunction. To proceed without notice was an exceptional course that should only be followed with good reason. Consequently, the Court could not entertain the claimant's application for orders prohibiting the use or disclosure of confidential information and enforcing the restrictive covenants. These applications should be dealt with at an inter partes hearing as there was no good reason why they should be heard without notice.

5.3. Applications with notice

5.3.1. An 'on notice' application will require giving the other party at least 3 clear days' notice and the relevant evidence must be served at the same time. Note however

(i) that as the specified period is 5 days or less, Saturday, Sunday and Bank Holidays do not count as clear days (see CPR rule 2.8(4));

(ii) that a document served after 4.30pm on a business day or at any time on a Saturday, Sunday or bank holiday is deemed to be served the next business day (see CPR rule 6.26).

5.4. The correct paperwork

5.4.1. The application is made through an application notice N16A (general Form of Application for injunction).

5.4.2. Under PD 25A it must be supported by evidence. This would normally be in a witness statement or statements although the evidence can technically be in the notice or in a statement of case, if verified by a statement of truth. The relevant documentary evidence will be exhibited to the witness statement(s). It will normally be necessary also to issue and serve a claim form. This is considered in more detail below.

5.4.3. The application notice must also be accompanied by a draft of the order sought.

5.5. Where and when to lodge the paperwork

Service on the other party

5.5.1. An application for an injunction must be served on the other party as soon as possible and in any event, not less than three days before the court is to hear the application (PD 25A para 2). Permission to serve on shorter notice would have to be obtained from the Interim Applications Judge if in the Chancery Division (Chancery Guide para 16.9) or from a Master in the Queen's Bench Division (QB Guide para 13.1.6).

5.5.2. Service can be by various methods but is most commonly by post or (to ensure that there is evidence of service) by personal service. It can also be by email, although note that if the issued claim form is also being served, there are various conditions applying to service by email (see PD 6A).

Filing in Queen's Bench

5.5.3. To issue the claim form, take or send the claim form N1, and the relevant fee, to Room E07, Action Department, Central Office, Royal Courts of Justice, Strand, London, WC2A 2LL. For further details, number of copies etc. see QB Guide para 4.1.5.

5.5.4. The application notice for an on notice injunction should be filed at the Listing Office, Room WG 08, for a hearing to be listed. The QB Guide says this applies where a claim "has been started".

5.5.5. If the application is to be made without giving notice to the other parties, the application notice stamped with the appropriate fee should be brought to Court 37 (The Interim Applications Court) together with evidence in support, a skeleton argument and two copies of the order sought. Urgent applications are heard at 10am and 2pm and such other times as the urgency dictates (QB Guide para 14.2).

Filing in Chancery Division

5.5.6. The claim form should be issued in the Rolls Buildings or in a District Registry of the High Court. The Rolls Buildings address is 7 Rolls Buildings, Fetter Lane, London EC4A 1NL.

5.5.7. The application notice and appropriate fee should be taken to Judge's Listing, accompanied by a completed "Judge's Application Form" (Chancery Guide para 16.9). It will then only be heard if two copies of the claim form and further copies of the application notice are served on Judge's Listing before 12 noon on the day before the hearing date.

5.5.8. If the application is likely to take longer than 2 hours it should not be listed before the interim applications judge: in this event, Judge's Listing should be notified immediately.

The bundle

5.5.9. In addition to initially lodging the paperwork at court, a bundle of documents must be prepared for the application hearing if the documents to be referred to total 25 pages or more. This should be agreed where possible. The QB Guide does not appear to specify when this must be lodged in a hearing before a judge, but it would be safe to follow the rule which applies in a hearing before a master where it would be lodged 1 to 3 days prior to the hearing (see QB Guide 12.3).

County Court

5.5.10. In the County Court, both the claim form and the application notice must be lodged at the relevant county court office. This can be at any court centre.

5.6.   Paying the fee

5.6.1. There is a separate fee to issue the application notice and (if applicable) to issue the claim.

   (i)   The relevant court fees are to be found at Schedule 1 to the Civil Proceedings Fees Order 2008 (SI 2008/1053) as amended[1].

   (ii) The fee to make an application on notice is normally £255 (Schedule 1, 2.4(a)).

   (iii) To issue a claim for an injunction, where there is and will be no claim for a sum of money, the relevant court fee is £528 in the High Court and £308 in the County Court (Schedule 1, 1.5).

---

1   The figures stated below are correct as at March 2020

(iv) Where the value of the claim exceeds £10,000 but does not exceed £200,000, the claim issue fee is 5% of the value of the claim (Schedule 1, 1.1).

(v) Where proceedings are started in the High Court or County Court and the claim exceeds £200,000 or is not limited, the relevant fee to issue the claim is £10,000 (Schedule 1, 1.1).

(vi) Where the claimant does not identify the value of the claim when starting proceedings to recover a sum of money, the fee payable to issue the claim is the one applicable to a claim where the sum is not limited.

5.7.   Is there a need for proceedings to be issued / for particulars of claim before or at the time of an injunction application?

5.7.1. This is a question of practical importance for claimants, not least because the issue fee (generally 5% of the value of the claim) has to be paid for the claim to be issued.

5.7.2. Practice Direction 25A covers "Urgent applications and applications without notice" and provides as follows:

4.1 These fall into two categories:

(1) applications where a claim form has already been issued, and

(2) applications where a claim form has not yet been issued,

and, in both cases, where notice of the application has not been given to the respondent.

4.2 These applications are normally dealt with at a court hearing but cases of extreme urgency may be dealt with by telephone.

4.3 Applications dealt with at a court hearing after issue of a claim form:

(1) the application notice, evidence in support and a draft order (as in 2.4 above) should be filed with the court two hours before the hearing wherever possible,

(2) if an application is made before the application notice has been issued, a draft order (as in 2.4 above) should be provided at the hearing, and the application notice and evidence in support must be filed with the court on the same or next working day or as ordered by the court, and

(3) except in cases where secrecy is essential, the applicant should take steps to notify the respondent informally of the application.

4.4 Applications made before the issue of a claim form:

(1) in addition to the provisions set out at 4.3 above, unless the court orders otherwise, either the applicant must undertake to the court to issue a claim form immediately or the court will give directions for the commencement of the claim,

(2) where possible the claim form should be served with the order for the injunction.

5.7.3.   PD 25A para 5.1(5)(a) provides that an order for an injunction must, if made before issue of a claim form, contain an undertaking to issue and pay the appropriate fee on the next working day, or directions for commencement of the claim.

5.7.4.   It follows that it is possible to issue an application notice without issuing proceedings but if so, the court will order the claim form to be issued/served straight away. Technically, following the issue of a claim form the claimant would have 4 months to file the Particulars of Claim, but it is likely to be needed much sooner than this.

5.7.5. Best practice is to issue the claim, with Particulars of Claim, at the same time as the Application Notice. The next best option would be to issue the claim with Particulars to follow.

5.7.6. In *Caterpillar Logistics v Huesca de Crean* [2012] EWCA Civ 156 the Court of Appeal (Stanley Burnton LJ) strongly criticised the fact that the claimant had not served Particulars of Claim until after the return date for the interim injunction and (in fact) outside the time limit under the CPR.

> *"If the timetable provided by the CPR had been followed by CLS in this action these proceedings could have been ready for trial on the date which was ultimately fixed for the return date namely 9 November 2011, or so nearly ready that a speedy trial could have been ordered within the next few weeks... Mr Bloch told the judge that it was normal practice in claims for confidentiality injunctions for the service of Particulars of Claim to be deferred until after the application for an interim injunction has been dealt with. If that is the normal practice, I consider that it should be discontinued. Like Tugendhat J, I consider that it is in the interests of justice and the efficient and fair conduct of proceedings that the claimant's case be defined and pleaded as soon as possible, so that the defendant knows precisely what is the case against her, and so does the judge. That is particularly the case where, as here, allegations of misconduct are made against a defendant."*

5.8. Skeleton arguments

5.8.1. Skeleton arguments/draft orders etc. may be sent to the court by email (Chancery Guide para 6.9/ QB Guide para 12.3.7).

5.8.2. The skeleton argument "for substantial applications..." should be served not later than 1 day before the hearing in the Listing

Office. Where a skeleton argument is provided by email a hard copy should be brought to the hearing. Parties should avoid handing each other skeletons at the door of the court so each party has time to consider them (QB Guide 12.3).

5.8.3.　On a without notice application, the skeleton argument should be submitted to the applications court along with the other paperwork (QB Guide 14.2).

5.8.4.　In the Chancery Division it is a requirement that every skeleton argument should begin with an estimate of the time required for pre-reading and the time required in court (Chancery Guide para 16.16). In the Queen's Bench Division the skeleton argument should contain a reading list and an estimate of the time it will take the judge to read it (QB Guide 12.3.8).

5.9.　Joining other Defendants

5.9.1.　It is often desirable to bring a claim both against the departing employee(s) and against the company s/he now works for, or the company s/he has created. This is often done by means of the economic torts and in particular:

(i)　inducement of breach of contract,

(ii)　unlawful interference with economic interests, and

(iii) civil conspiracy.

5.9.2.　The law relating to these common law torts is complex and extensive and will be dealt with here by way of a brief overview.

5.9.3.　If the employees have gone to work for a competitor, that competitor and other third parties might well be liable for inducing a breach of their contract as long as they had the requisite knowledge and carried out the relevant inducement.

5.9.4. The tort depends on knowledge by the defendant that s/he is inducing a breach. The knowledge of the directors will be imputed to a company. Hence, whilst the defendant must knowingly induce the breach of contract, the definition can be satisfied even if the defendant was not motivated by malice but motivated, for example, by economic gain (ie. there is still liability if the inducement was merely a means to another end, such as setting up in competition). Nevertheless, an honest belief that there is no breach of contract will excuse the defendant. Importantly, liability for inducing breach of contract requires that the person who induced the breach of contract should have actual knowledge of the contract and intend to procure a breach of it. It is not enough that this person ought reasonably to have been aware of the contract: "[n]egligent interference is not actionable". It does not however matter if the relevant defendant did not know the precise terms of the contract: see *OBG v Allen* [2007] UKHL 21 (linked with *Douglas v Hello* [2007] 2 WLR 920).

5.9.5. The case of *Re-Use Collections v Sendall*, which is discussed in detail above, points to one limitation to causes of action based on inducement of breach. The Court found that the company the claimant set up as a vehicle for competing could not be liable for inducing breach of his contract, not least because the claimant had formed an intention to breach his contract long before the company was set up so inducement could not be shown. However, the company was properly made a defendant to a claim of unlawful means conspiracy notwithstanding that the claimant was its controlling mind.

5.9.6. The other cause of action which is commonly relied on is the tort of unlawful interference with another person's economic interests. Unlawful interference consists of intentionally damaging another person's business by unlawful means. Both the unlawful means and intention elements are key although another necessary element is interfering with the freedom of a third party to deal with the claimant. Potentially this could be satisfied by the act of 'stealing' clients from a business. This tort was also considered in detail in *OBG v Allen* where Lord Hoffman said "[o]ne intends to cause loss even though it is the means by which one achieved the end of enriching oneself". In other words, the defendant can intend the damage to the business only as a means to another end, such as advancing the defendant's economic interests. However, for these purposes it is not enough that loss to the claimant is merely foreseeable.

5.9.7. Conspiracy is an agreement or understanding between two or more parties to do an unlawful act, or to do an unlawful act by unlawful means: *Mulcahy v R* (1868) LR 3 HL 306. There are two types of civil conspiracy:

(i) the first is 'lawful means' conspiracy, which does not involve the commission of an unlawful act but the sole or predominant purpose is to injure someone; this type of conspiracy will be rare in employee competition cases, where the predominant intention is normally personal gain rather than the injury of another;

(ii) the second is 'unlawful means' conspiracy, where the agreed course of action or the means involved are unlawful, because, for example, they involve a tort such as inducing breach of contract; this also involves an agreement to injure someone by unlawful means but it does not need to be the predominant purpose.

5.9.8. For the tort of conspiracy to be made out, there is no need for an express agreement. Further, it is not necessary for all the conspirators to join the conspiracy at the same time. Where this cause of action is relied upon in an employee competition case, the argument often focuses on the mental element. For these purposes, it would be enough if a company agreed with individuals who were employed by someone else that they would do something which would breach the express or implied terms of their contracts of employment: there is no need to show that it was the company's predominant intention to injure the current employer. A 'predominant intention to injure' is not necessary: per *Lonrho plc v Fayed* [1991] 1 AC 448.

CHAPTER SIX
WHAT HAPPENS AT THE INTERLOCUTORY HEARING?

6.1. The test to be applied by the court: *American Cyanamid*

6.1.1. The principles in *American Cyanamid* [1975] AC 396 apply (see in particular pp407B and 408G):

(a) The court must be satisfied that there is a serious question to be tried. Unless the material fails to disclose that the claimant has any real prospect of succeeding, the court should go on to consider the balance of convenience. On this test the court will not look at the merits of each party's case. There will be a serious issue unless the claimant's position is manifestly hopeless.

(b) An injunction will not normally be granted if the applicant would be adequately compensated by an award of damages at trial.

(c) The claimant's undertaking in damages must be adequate compensation for the defendant in the event that it is required to compensate the defendant for any loss caused by the injunction if it later transpires that the injunction was wrongly granted.

(d) Where the balance of convenience lies between the parties will be an important factor in deciding whether to grant an injunction.

(e) Where other factors are evenly balanced it is a counsel of prudence to take such measures as are calculated to preserve the status quo.

6.1.2. Whilst Lord Diplock's guidance above is of great authority, it is not to be read as a statute. In practice it is applied with some degree of flexibility.

6.1.3. As to the fourth factor, the balance of convenience, *Affinity Workplace Solutions v McCann* [2019] EWHC 2839 (Ch) provides a good recent example of a case where the balance of convenience test ultimately determined the case in the employees' favour, despite the existence of an arguably enforceable PTR. Prior to the court proceedings, the claimant had sought to restrain four ex-employees by drawing up lists of prohibited clients and seeking undertakings, but then changed tack and sought an injunction, in part on the basis of a non-competition clause which ran for six months and which they had not referred to before. The Court accepted that if the claimant could establish a serious issue that there was a binding PTR, the starting point would be that an injunction would be granted. However, there was a real prospect an injunction would not be granted as for a significant period the claimant had pursued a remedy via undertakings without making reference to the covenant and the listing of clients suggested that that alone might have been enough to protect its legitimate interests. As by the time of the injunction the employees had been allowed to become established in a new position, the balance of convenience favoured no injunction being granted.

6.1.4. It is also important to qualify Lord Diplock's second factor: an injunction should not be granted if "damages would be an adequate remedy". Whilst it may appear that damages are always adequate, in practice the courts regard unlawful competition as a situation where the true extent of loss will be difficult to establish. In *D v P* [2016] IRLR 355 the claimant had not claimed damages but only an injunction to restrain the defendant from taking up a position with a rival. The Court of Appeal said:

(i) damages "will usually be unquantifiable and will rarely, if ever, provide the covenantee with an adequate substitute for an injunction";

(ii) absence of damage to the claimant is not in general a bar to relief save where there is exceptional prejudice or hardship to a defendant;

(iii) the starting point in the consideration of a claim by an employer to enforce an employee's negative covenant is an injunction.

6.2.   When will the merits at trial be considered on an interim injunction application?

6.2.1.   Where the grant or refusal of an interlocutory injunction will effectively end the action, it is appropriate for the court in assessing the balance of convenience to investigate "the degree of likelihood" of the claimant succeeding at trial (*WNL v Woods* [1979] 1 WLR 1294 p1306). This suggests that the test is simply whether the injunction will finally dispose of the action. In fact the test is slightly more nuanced.

> "It is only if the action cannot be tried before the period of the restraint has expired, or has run a large part of its course, that the grant of the interlocutory injunction will effectively dispose of the action, thus bringing the case within the exception to the rule in American Cyanamid, such as was considered by the House of Lords in N.W.L. Ltd. v. Woods... It is then that the judge may properly go on to consider the prospects of the employers succeeding in the action. Another way of reaching the same conclusion is to say that the longer the period of the interlocutory injunction, the more likely it is that the employee may suffer damage (if the injunction is wrongly granted) which is uncompensatable by the employers on their cross-undertaking, and therefore it becomes necessary to consider the relative strength of each party's case as revealed by the affidavit*

evidence.." Lawrence David v Ashton [1991] 1 All ER 385 p.153A

6.2.2. *Niit Technologies Ltd v Chaturvedi* (High Court QB 10.3.17) provides a recent example. The restraints lasted for 12 months of which 6 had already run by the time of the injunction application in early March 2017. It was established that the Court could hear a speedy trial by June, by which time 9 months would have run. The Judge accepted that the "serious issue to be tried" test did not apply in those circumstances, and he needed to consider the merits.

6.2.3. The question of whether the merits can be considered was reconsidered by the Court of Appeal in *Forse v Secarma* [2019] EWCA Civ 215 in the context of springboard relief (springboard relief and springboard injunctions are explained in detail Chapter 10). The fourth and fifth defendants were companies offering penetration testing services, which involves testing and exposing weaknesses in the IT systems of clients. They outsourced this work to the claimant companies. The claimants alleged that their former directors, the first and second defendants, whilst bound by PTRs, had unlawfully conspired to poach their employees to start an in-house penetration testing team in the fourth and fifth defendant companies. The claimants sought and obtained a springboard injunction. The defendants submitted that the judge had erred in finding that damages were not an adequate remedy, the injunction was too wide and that it punished the defendants.

6.2.4. Between March and November 2018, 28 employees left to join the fourth and fifth defendants. The claimants obtained an interim springboard injunction on 30 November, based on an unlawful means conspiracy to set up a rival whilst the defendants were still employed. This prevented the first and second defendants or any of the claimant's ex-employees from providing services to the fourth and fifth defendants. It was to continue until the expedited trial listed on 1 April 2019. The matter came to the Court of Appeal on 13 March 2019.

6.2.5. The Court noted that a springboard injunction "*effectively delivers to the claimant, in advance of the trial, all or part of the substantive relief which the claimant seeks*". They said that save only where the time gap between the application for interim relief and the trial is insignificant, on applications for an interim springboard injunction the court should assess and take into account the strength of each side's case both as regards liability and also the length of time during which any unfair advantage from the springboard will continue (see para 34 ibid.).

6.2.6. This is an important case as it moves the point in time at which the court's duty to consider the merits is triggered in cases involving springboard injunctions. The duty to consider the merits does not only arise where there will be no trial until the restraint has expired or has run a large part of its course (per *Lawrence David* above): rather, the Court says the merits should be considered *except* where the gap between injunction and trial is *insignificant* [emphasis added]. Helpfully, the judgment goes on to talk about the manner in which the merits should be considered:

> "*In carrying out that exercise, the judge cannot conduct a detailed mini trial on disputed evidence. He or she must, however, undertake a fair and reasonable evaluation of the evidence bearing in mind that there will have been no disclosure, and the witness evidence will be incomplete and untested by cross-examination.*" (para 34)

6.2.7. In *Forse*, relying heavily on Whatsapp messages showing the plan to move the whole team to set up in competition, the Court found that the evidence strongly supported an unlawful means conspiracy and the springboard injunction was rightly granted. It was noted that the injunction would give the claimants time to persuade ex-employees to rejoin, to recruit new employees and secure other resources to remove unfair competitive advantage.

6.3. The outcome of the interlocutory hearing

6.3.1. Assuming the claimant wins and the matter has not been dealt with by consent on the basis of undertakings, the Judge will make an order for an injunction and decide the question of costs.

6.3.2. Directions to take the matter to trial will also be given at the hearing.

6.3.3. Even where there is to be a trial in the near future, costs may well be awarded against the losing party at the interim stage and they may be summarily assessed. By way of example, this happened in the recent case of *Ropner Insurance Services v Wood and Clearwood International* (QB) LTL 7/12/16, an application based on prior breaches of confidentiality and the breach of a 12-month non-competition covenant by an insurance broker. The case shows:

- the fact a departing employee may be prevented from continuing in business following departure is not an adequate reason for refusing an injunction at the interim stage, even where evidence showed he had limited financial means;

- the draconian effect of summary costs assessment at an interim injunction hearing; £21,000 costs were awarded against the defendant at the interim hearing, though he was effectively unemployed.

6.4. Penal notice

6.4.1. An order made at the hearing, whether involving an injunction or undertakings by consent, will need to contain a penal notice, spelling out the effect of breaching the order. A typical form of such notice is set out here:

....

PENAL NOTICE

Name and address of the Defendant:
XXXXXXXXXX OF [address].

IF YOU THE WITHIN NAMED XXXXXXXXXX DISOBEY THE UNDERTAKINGS GIVEN IN THIS ORDER YOU MAY BE HELD TO BE IN CONTEMPT OF COURT AND LIABLE TO IMPRISONMENT OR FINED OR YOUR ASSETS SEIZED

ANY OTHER PERSON WHO KNOWS OF THE UNDER-TAKINGS GIVEN IN THIS ORDER AND DOES ANYTHING WHICH HELPS OR PERMITS THE DEFENDANT TO BREACH THE TERMS OF THIS ORDER MAY BE HELD TO BE IN CON-TEMPT OF COURT AND MAY BE IMPRISONED, FINED OR HAVE THEIR ASSETS SEIZED.

IMPORTANT

NOTICE TO THE DEFENDANT

(1)   This Order contains undertakings that prohibit you from doing the acts set out in Schedule A to this Order. You should read it all carefully. You have a right to ask the Court to vary or discharge this Order.

(2)   If you disobey the undertakings set out in Schedule A to this Order you may be found guilty of Contempt of Court and you may be sent to prison or your assets may be seized.

....

6.5. Directions

6.5.1. In other respects, directions will generally be needed for the matter to proceed to trial. If orders have been made for the forensic examination of computers, the detailed provisions will need to be set out and probably a further return date will be necessary once the outcome of the examination is known.

6.5.2. In the interests of speed, it may be worth providing that the court dispenses with the requirement for a listing questionnaire and pre-trial checklists unless the Listing Officer directs otherwise.

6.6. Costs budgets

6.6.1. Even if the case is due for speedy trial, the claim will be subject to the costs budgeting regime of the CPR and the filing of precedent H and agreeing of costs budgets (with a costs case management hearing) will need to be included in the directions.

6.6.2. It is important also to note the possibility of providing in the directions, pursuant to CPR rule 3.12, that the case will not be costs managed, and the parties need not file or exchange costs budgets. The judge would need to be persuaded that this is the right course to take.

6.7. Speedy trials

6.7.1. Consider an application for a speedy trial. The court has the power to fix the date under its general powers: see CPR r. 29.2(2), and to expedite any hearing date: CPR r. 3.1(2(b).

6.7.2. Judicial commentary has been supportive of speedy trials in restrictive covenant cases but see *Ifone Ltd v. Davies* [2005] EWHC 1504 (Ch): Laddie J commented that the court should not order an expedited trial unless it was convinced that there were pressing reasons to justify that course. They are often necessary in employee competition cases because:

- the effect of the injunction or undertakings impedes the defendant's ability to earn a living until the issues are determined;

- if the trial does not get on quickly, disputed restrictive covenants will have run their course, rendering the trial pointless.

CHAPTER SEVEN
USING THE COURT PROCESS TO FIND OUT WHAT THE EX-EMPLOYEE HAS DONE

Disclosure orders, delivery up orders, search orders, and examination of computers

7.1. Getting disclosure on the interim application

7.1.1. Given the need for urgency in interim injunctions, formal applications to court for pre-action disclosure prior to the hearing of the application are rarely appropriate. Under the CPR an application for pre-action disclosure may only be made:

  (i) where the applicant and respondent are likely to be parties to the proceedings (see CPR r. 31.16(3)(a));

  (ii) if proceedings had been started, where the respondent's duty by way of standard disclosure would extend to the document or class of document of which pre-action disclosure is sought (see CPR r. 31.16(3)(b), and (c)); and

  (iii) so long as disclosure before proceedings have started is "desirable in order to dispose fairly of the anticipated proceedings, assist the dispute to be resolved without proceedings or save costs." (see CPR r. 31.16(3)(d)).

7.1.2. It is much more common for the same result to be sought as an order for information about clients approached or about information removed within the terms of an interlocutory injunction.

7.1.3. An extreme example of the kind of information which a claimant employer might obtain by these means is illustrated in the decision of Nicholas Warren QC (sitting as a Deputy High Court Judge) in *Intelsec Systems & Ors v. Grech-Cini & Ors* [2000] 1 WLR 1190, a case involving allegations that a former employee had used names and addresses of business contacts. The employer applied successfully for interim relief including an order that the defendants disclose the names and addresses of all persons with whom they had been in contact both whilst employed by it and since the commencement of the new employment with a view to supplying or soliciting orders, regardless of whether they had been clients of the claimant or not. This was subject to the condition that post employment it was disclosed only to the claimant's solicitors and not to the claimant without an order from the court. However, this is a surprising result and it will not be repeated readily as it is a mandatory injunction requiring disclosure of information at a very early stage. In *Aon v JLT* [2000] 1 WLR 1190, the High Court said that such orders would be exceptional. There will often be a strong argument that it is not needed at an early stage and can await the stage of standard disclosure being reached.

7.1.4. It is not uncommon for a claimant to seek an affidavit from the defendant(s), as part of the interim order, setting out the use they have made of the confidential information. Note *Dorma v Bateman & Ors* [2016] IRLR 616 in which the claimant applied for such an affidavit. The Judge said that it had been appropriate to ask but said it was not necessary because the information requested had already been provided in the defendants' witness statements and if that proved to be false, the remedy of committal for contempt would be available.

7.2. Search orders

7.2.1. Search orders, previously known as *Anton Piller* orders, require the respondent to the order to admit the applicant to their premises for the purposes of preserving evidence or property which might otherwise be destroyed or hidden. Self-evidently, this is a draconian order which is only likely to be sought in an employee competition case in the clearest of circumstances. The application would be made without notice and the threshold is that "there is grave danger of property being smuggled away or of vital evidence being destroyed" (per Lord Denning in *Anton Piller KG v Manufacturing Processes Ltd* [1976] Ch 55). The onerous requirements which an applicant must satisfy to obtain such an order and the possibility of obtaining lesser forms of order, such as a delivery up order or orders permitting the examination of computers, means that today their use in employee competition cases is relatively rare. In the circumstances, no more than a brief overview will be given here.

7.2.2. The power to make such an order comes from section 7 of the Civil Procedure Act 1997 which allows an order to be granted for the purpose of preserving evidence which may be relevant to the proceedings. The application is made pursuant to CPR rule 25.1(1)(h) and Practice Direction 25A – Interim Injunctions. There are various conditions to be satisfied including the duty of full and frank disclosure. If the order is granted, an independent Supervising Solicitor must be appointed to personally serve the order and supervise the search, unless the court orders otherwise.

7.2.3. A common variation of the standard order is to provide for disk imaging of computers. This has various repercussions. First, an order permitting a search of someone's devices without notice is no easier to obtain than a physical search order, as it is a serious invasion of privacy and it may engage Article 8 of the European Convention on Human Rights. Secondly, a computer disk may contain material which is subject to legal professional privilege and this must not be permitted to come into the hands of the applicant or their solicitor. The respondent may be involved in removing such material by agreement with the supervising solicitor. Thirdly, an independent computer specialist will need to be appointed to supervise the imaging, in a role similar to that of the supervising solicitor.

7.3.   Delivery up orders

7.3.1. These subdivide into "doorstep delivery up orders" and simple "delivery up orders".

7.3.2. A doorstep delivery up order would be applied for without notice and requires the immediate delivery up of documents to a solicitor standing on the doorstep of the respondent. The courts have said that there is little difference between this and a full search order and therefore similar safeguards might need to be put in place, including the involvement of a supervising solicitor: see in particular *Adam Phones v Goldschmidt* [1999] 4 All ER 486. It is a requirement of CPR 25A PD 8.2 that consideration is given by the court to whether, for the protection of parties, similar provisions should be put in place to those used in a search order. In general, such an order must permit legal advice to be taken by the party against whom the order is made, at the point when the order is executed and before complying with it.

7.3.3. The other type of delivery up order simply requires property and documents to be handed over within a reasonable period of time, in practice often by the defendant delivering them to the claimant's solicitor's office. Whilst CPR 25A PD 8.2 still applies, the court is unlikely to apply the onerous requirements of a search order. The traditional basis for such an order is section 4 of the Torts (Interference with Goods) Act 1977 which applies to the delivery up of goods which are or may become the subject matter of proceedings. However, electronically stored information will not fall within this definition. One answer to this difficulty may be provided by the Copyright Designs and Patents Act 1988 and the Copyright and Rights in Databases Regulations 1997, which provide for delivery up as an interim remedy.

7.3.4. Whilst the delivery up of a wrongfully taken database may provide the necessary relief, an applicant could further or alternatively seek the destruction of confidential information held in electronic form. This is also likely to require permission for an independent computer expert to access the relevant devices and a copy of all such information being held pending trial.

7.3.5. *Hyperama Plc v Poulis* [2018] EWHC 3483 (QB) illustrates the hurdles which a claimant needs to get over to obtain a doorstep delivery up order without notice. The claimant was a food wholesaler. The defendants had been employees. The claimant sought both hard copy documents and electronic documents. The claimant contended they had taken confidential information with the intention of unlawfully competing with the claimant, were in breach of PTRs and had acted fraudulently by diverting secret profits whilst in employment. Pepperall J suggested that what was sought was a variation of a search order and an elevated standard applied such that he needed a high degree of assurance that the claims would succeed at trial, albeit he accepted that less was required to justify a doorstep order than a search order.

7.3.6. He said that for a successful application he would also require the following: (1) the potential/ actual damage to the business must be very serious; (2) there should be clear evidence that incriminating documents were in the defendant's possession; (3) there should be a real possibility that they might destroy the material before the *inter partes* hearing; (4) the relief must be proportionate to the claimant's legitimate aims.

7.3.7. He decided the case justified only a delivery up order limited to electronic documents in which there was no entry upon the defendant's premises, no need for any search for hard copies and no entitlement for the claimant to see anything until after the *inter partes* hearing. He said a search order would not have been justified.

7.3.8. In *Wild Brain Family International v (1) Robson & (2) Chubb* [2018] EWHC 3163 (Ch) the Court had to decide whether a doorstep delivery up order and a computer imaging order were properly made without notice. The doorstep order required the defendants immediately on service of the order to deliver up to the claimant's solicitors copies of the claimant's confidential information and documents. The imaging order required them to allow an independent computer specialist to copy all the data stored on their computer equipment after a certain date, albeit an order to inspect those documents was not being applied for at this stage.

7.3.9. The Judge (HHJ Klein, sitting as a Judge of the High Court) rejected the defendants' submission that it was neither here nor there that the order did not permit them to enter the defendants' homes. In this respect what was being sought was distinguished from a search order but a search of an individual's virtual life (by taking copies of data for example) was almost as intrusive. The Judge said the more intrusive the order sought, the higher the burden and in an appropriate case, the test which the court is required to apply for a search order may be adopted even though only inspection and no search of premises was being sought. He said that before the Court could make a delivery up order or search order without notice, he must be satisfied that there was a "real possibility" of destruction of documents. This test was met in the instant case.

7.4. Examination of computers

7.4.1. This section deals with computer imaging and inspection orders which might be ordered at the same 'on notice' interim relief hearing at which an injunction is sought. Such an order would be made under CPR rule 25.1(1)(c)(i) which applies to the detention, preservation and inspection of relevant property.

7.4.2. In recent years, a more permissive approach appears to have been adopted by the courts when considering applications for the imaging and inspection of computers. Consequently, it is increasingly common for claimants to obtain orders allowing experts to examine computers to find confidential information which has been improperly retained or transferred by the defendant. However, it is important to emphasise that these are a form of mandatory injunction and when such orders are made the court will often place strict controls around how computers are accessed and what may be done with the information. The development of the court's approach will now be considered.

7.4.3. The primary concerns of the courts when faced with such applications are to avoid interfering with the defendant's Article 8 right to privacy and also to ensure access is not granted to information which may be covered by legal professional privilege. These must be balanced against any denial of justice to the claimant at the particular stage in the proceedings.

7.4.4. The following list of relevant factors in determining whether an order was necessary and proportionate was given by Akenhead J in *McLennan Architects Ltd v Jones* [2014] EWHC 2604 (TCC)[1]:

(a) The scope of the investigation must be proportionate.

(b) The investigation must be limited to what is reasonably necessary.

(c) Regard should be had for the likely contents of the device sought so that any search should exclude possible disclosure of privileged documents or documents irrelevant to the case.

(d) Regard should be had to the human rights of those whose information is on the device and the relevance of any such information to the case.

---

1 *McLennan Architects* was not an employee competition case, but the principles are of general application.

(e) Access to a complete hard drive would rarely be granted unless dedicated to a particular contract or project.

(f) The court should require a confidentiality undertaking from any expert or other person given access to the relevant electronic devices.

7.4.5. In *McLennan Architects*, by the time of the hearing, Akenhead J considered the proposed order had been limited in scope to what was 'sensible and proportionate,' overcoming objections to what had earlier been sought. By that stage the inspection sought was limited to four emails and it was agreed the IT consultant would be appointed by the defendant.

7.4.6. It is possible to discern two strands in the authorities, one strand applying a more restrictive approach and one a more permissive one. The more permissive cases tend to approach the question on the basis of the test for an interim injunction where the key issue is the balance of convenience between the parties.

Cases suggesting a more restrictive approach

7.4.7. The 'necessary and proportionate' requirement was applied in *Phaestos Ltd v Ho* [2012] EWHC 1375 (TCC), which is a helpful case to understand the approach of the courts. In that case, the claimant was concerned that former employees had taken and used its software. Amongst other things, it applied for an order for delivery up of the claimant's confidential information, an order requiring the imaging of the defendants' electronic storage devices and an order for searches of those images to establish whether the software had been taken and if so whether it had been used. The claimants submitted it was necessary to carry out a search of the images for two reasons: (1) to police the defendants' delivery up and disclosure obligations (2) to obtain evidence of the extent of the defendants' wrongdoing. The Judge held that the claimant was entitled to the orders for delivery up and imaging. The latter was justified on the basis that it was necessary for the purpose of preserving evidence. However, he held that there should be no order for the searching of the images.

7.4.8. He applied both the tests under CPR 31, which relates to specific disclosure, and CPR 25.1 which relates to orders for preservation and inspection of property. First, he held that the order for imaging was not necessary to police disclosure of documents relevant to pleaded issues. To order it would be to preempt the procedures for e-disclosure. Further, the nature of the search the claimant proposed to carry out was such that it did not appear the claimant was really seeking to inspect disclosable documents within the meaning of CPR 31. Rather, they were attempting to police the defendant's obligation to deliver up the claimant's property and find evidence of its misuse. The inspection was not necessary to police the delivery up orders because the delivery up process had not yet been completed. Any complaint about delivery up should be part of a fresh application to court once the process was complete.

7.4.9. Finally, inspection was not necessary to preserve and identify relevant evidence of the nature and extent of the already pleaded wrongdoing (either under CPR 25.1 or by virtue of the court's inherent jurisdiction). In rejecting the necessity of the order on this basis, the Judge was attentive to the fact that the claimant's principal claim was for delivery up and not for the commercial misuse of its property. The proposed order for inspection on the other hand was, in the opinion of the Judge, in large part sought in order to obtain evidence that the defendants had misused the claimant's property or wrongfully disclosed it to third parties. Since there was no evidence of such misuse before the Judge and since there was no pleaded case to that effect, the application for inspection was in truth 'an unjustified fishing expedition' and therefore unnecessary.

7.4.10. In *CBS Butler v Brown & Ors* [2013] EWHC 3944 (QB), the claimant, having already obtained an order for imaging of relevant storage devices for the purpose of "preserving" relevant evidence, made a further application seeking to allow its own IT expert to use keyword searches for disclosable material, whilst blacklisting search terms for information that should not be disclosed because of privilege. The Court refused the application. By the time of the hearing, a defence had been filed and disclosure would happen in due course. The order was 'intrusive,' 'contrary to normal principles of justice' and could only be made 'when there is a paramount need to prevent a denial of justice to the claimant.' The Judge said that such a denial of justice may be shown after the defendant has failed to comply with its disclosure obligations or before disclosure has been required where the claimant can show 'substantial reasons' for believing the defendant is intending to breach his disclosure obligations. The fact that the defendant has misused confidential information or is in breach of his employment contract will not be sufficient to demonstrate this intention.

7.4.11. However, it should be noted that the high threshold set in this case may have been influenced by the fact that had the order been granted, it would have denied the defendant any involvement in the inspection process, thereby rendering it particularly intrusive.

Cases suggesting a more permissive approach

7.4.12. In *Warm Zones v Thurley* [2014] IRLR 791, the claimant brought proceedings against the new employer of two of its former employees, which led them to discover email exchanges between the defendant and the ex-employees suggesting the latter had misused confidential information whilst still in the claimant's employment. The claimant successfully sought interim relief against the employees consisting of an order for imaging and inspection of their computers by a specialist.

7.4.13. Simler J applied the usual principles when determining a mandatory interim injunction. The order could therefore only be granted if it carried the least risk of injustice if it turned out to be wrong. The Court would have to feel a high degree of assurance that the claimant would establish its right at trial. There was strong prima facie evidence of misuse of the claimant's database by the defendants during the course of their employment.

7.4.14. When considering the balance of convenience, Simler J placed significance on the fact that the order sought was 'a focused one, designed simply to secure the return, protection and security of its confidential information.' Further, the claimant made a commitment to 'provide safeguards in respect of any client confidential or third-party data on the defendant's computer' that did not belong to it.

7.4.15. The *Warm Zones* case should be treated with some caution. Simler J does not cite any of the aforementioned cases and gives no separate consideration to the necessary and proportionate requirement. She therefore does not consider whether the claimant's concerns regarding the potential misuse of its confidential information might have been met by less intrusive orders such as, for example, an order restraining the use of confidential information combined with an order for imaging of the devices.

7.4.16. A similarly permissive approach was taken in *AJG v Skriptchenko* [2016] EWHC 603 (QB). In that case, the claimant brought proceedings against two defendants, who had left to join a competitor, and obtained delivery up of their electronic devices and computer systems for inspection by the claimant's experts. This revealed that further employees should be defendants. The claimant sought a mandatory injunction for the search of devices and deletion of any confidential material which was found. As in *Warm Zones*, the Judge applied the principles usually applicable to applications for mandatory injunctive relief. In light of the defendants' behaviour, which had shown a "high degree of subterfuge," the Court felt a high degree of assurance that the claimant would succeed at trial but also that the defendants should not be left to delete the material themselves.

7.4.17. The order was granted on condition that a precise regime to identify the relevant documents was adopted: copies of all materials would be retained; any dispute as to whether material was confidential would be referred to the Judge; inspection and deletion was to be carried out by experts appointed by the defendants rather than the claimants, using agreed search terms; and the material need not be shown to the claimant if the defendant contended that it contained confidential information. However, disputed information was not to be available to the defendants until trial.

7.4.18. *Skriptchenko* should also be treated with caution. Again, Slade J cited none of the above cases (apart from *Warm Zones*) and does not seem to have applied the necessary and proportionate test. No explanation is given for why the mandatory order for destruction of the material could not have been given at the end of trial.

The recent cases

7.4.19. The more recent cases suggest that there has been a return to the orthodoxy of *McLennan Architects* and *CBS Butler*.

7.4.20. *WE Cox Claims Group Limited v Gavin Spencer* [2017] EWHC 2552 (QB) concerned the departure of the defendant from his position as a Managing Director and CEO of the claimant company. At some point before his resignation, the defendant took a copy of a list of the claimant's business contacts home on his external hard drive. On discovering what had happened, the claimant asked the defendant to confirm if he had used or copied the list. The defendant initially said that he had not, but later admitted that he had. The claimant sought an order for inspection by an independent IT consultant, instructed by both parties. The issue for the Judge was whether an order for inspection should not only attempt to establish whether the list was still on the defendant's hard drive, but whether it should look for any other of the claimant's confidential information.

7.4.21. The Judge applied the test in *CBS Butler* and considered the *McLennan* factors, observed that the claimant was seeking a 'strong order' that should only be made 'in special circumstances,' and concluded that the order could be granted in this case to allow the claimant to determine the extent of the confidential information taken. Relevant factors were: (1) the defendant had taken the list, copied it and made a secondary list (2) the defendant had not 'put all his cards on the table' when first asked about the list and (3) there was circumstantial evidence placing the defendant in 'enormous embarrassment.'

7.4.22. In *Hi-Level Enterprises Ltd v Levine* [2018] EWHC 1882 (Ch), the defendants had in principle accepted that there should be an order for inspection. The question for the Court was how intrusive the search should be. The claimant was proposing to carry out two searches. The first search was to use specified search terms to see if any of the claimant's database remained on the delivered-up devices and whether the defendants had, as they asserted, tried to delete it. The second search was to identify whether any parts of a database belonging to the claimant, which had been copied by the defendant, had been transferred onto any devices of the defendants that had not been delivered up or disclosed. In deciding this issue, the judge stated that the checklist of factors provided by Akenhead J in *McLennan Architects* for determining whether an order was necessary and proportionate was 'very helpful.' Further, the observation in *Cox* that any independent expert appointed to carry out a search 'needs to know exactly what it is that he is to do' was a valid one.

7.4.23. The proposed first search was sufficiently specific and could be granted. However, the judge accepted the defendants' objections to the second search: in particular, a provision in the proposed order that allowed the proposed specialist who was to carry out the search to 'take such sensible and proportionate steps to conduct the Search and Schedule A Search as is necessary' was impermissibly broad.

Costs implications of an imaging and inspection order

7.4.24. An argument frequently raised by defendants is that these orders give rise to disproportionate and open-ended costs awards. In *Cox*, the Judge acknowledged that the argument put forward on behalf of the defendants that the unknown and potentially considerable expense of the exercise should be a factor counting against the grant of an injunction was a 'strong' one. However, the Judge was mindful of the fact that an expert had quoted £3,600 plus VAT for looking at the list and above that, the parties would share the cost of the investigation, meaning that the claimant would have an incentive to minimize costs. Further, if, as the defendant contended, the only document he had copied was the list, then it seemed unlikely additional expense would be incurred. Finally, the defendant had only himself to blame for the fact that there had to be a wider search to satisfy the Court he had not taken other confidential information. In *Hi-Level Enterprises*, the defendant likewise made a complaint about open-ended costs but the Judge considered that the claimant's acceptance of a cap of £10,000 for the inspection was an acceptable response to this contention.

Conclusions

7.4.25. Five main points emerge from the case law in this area:

(i) Notwithstanding *Warm Zones* and *Skriptchenko*, it is most likely that applicants will have to convince the courts that the grant of such an order is necessary and proportionate. The *McLennan Architects* factors have been regarded as useful in determining this issue and were considered recently in *Cox* and *Hi-Level Enterprises*.

(ii) However, although the decisions in *Warm Zones* and *Skriptchenko* may be subject to scrutiny, it appears that it is now easier for claimants to obtain orders for the examination of computers and other electronic devices than it has been in the past (this may in large part be due to the fact that there are increasingly sophisticated ways to safeguard the confidential information of defendants and third parties).

(iii) There is a distinction between orders for imaging and for inspection. It will be much easier to obtain the former. In respect of the latter, the purpose for which inspection is sought and the stage proceedings have reached are relevant. For example, unjustified fishing expeditions before disclosure has taken place will not be looked upon favourably by the court. Often, inspection of the relevant material will not be allowed at the early stage of an interim injunction and will only be permitted shortly before trial.

(iv) If confidential material is to be deleted, it is more likely that such an order would not be made until the conclusion of trial. In any event it is essential that an image of the relevant hard drive is retained in case there are subsequent disputes.

(v) Real care will be needed in the drafting of any order sought and in devising a regime for inspection that is precise, proportionate and limited to what is reasonably necessary in the case.

CHAPTER EIGHT
THINGS THAT CAN GO WRONG – INDEMNITY COSTS AND COMMITTAL

8.1   Indemnity costs

8.1.1   There are two bases of assessment of costs: the standard basis and the indemnity basis. Under the latter, the requirement that the costs must be proportionate to the matters in issue is disapplied and any doubt as to whether costs were reasonably incurred is resolved in favour of the receiving party (CPR r.44.3(1), (3)).

8.1.2   The award of indemnity costs is usually reserved to cases where the court wishes to indicate disapproval of the conduct in the litigation of the party against whom costs are ordered. Unreasonable conduct to a high degree may be sufficient.

8.1.3   Indemnity costs could be awarded against a defendant who has flagrantly breached an order or misled the court or another party and might be awarded where a claimant takes an unnecessarily aggressive or precipitous approach to litigation, as the following examples show.

8.2   Awarded against Defendants

8.2.1   In the costs judgment which followed *QBE Management Services (UK) v Dymoke* [2012] IRLR 458 the Judge set out five principal reasons for awarding indemnity costs against Defendants (at para 20):

(a) the conduct was deserving of condemnation in that for many months the defendants were knowingly engaged in unlawful conduct aimed at acquiring their former employer's business by stealth without paying for it;

(b) they allowed their commercial interests to take precedence over the rights and wrongs of the situation;

(c) they dishonestly assured the claimant that they had complied with their obligations although disclosure showed a very different picture;

(d) they displayed a lack of candour with the Court at all stages;

(e) they persisted with their case notwithstanding that it was irreconcilable with their own contemporaneous documents.

8.3 <u>Awarded against Claimants</u>

8.3.1 An example of the type of conduct which might justify such an order against a claimant can be found in *Caterpillar Logistics v Huesca de Crean* [2012] EWCA Civ 156. This was an unsuccessful appeal against the strike out of proceedings for alleged pre-termination breaches on the basis that the claimant had no reasonable grounds for bringing the claim. The claimant had no evidence of any breach of contract or threatened breach of contract on the part of the defendant. The Judge said:

> *"I regard the conduct of CLS in deciding to bring proceedings against the respondent, without any prior complaint or attempt to see whether there was the basis of an amicable solution to its concerns, as wholly inappropriate. It is particularly appropriate for the possibilities of such a solution to be explored where there is on one side a large corporation and on the other a former employee whose annual salary would be a small fraction of the costs of litigation. Many defendants, faced*

with such a claim, would simply concede rather than risk bankruptcy. When CLS made its decision to bring proceedings, there could have been no assurance that QH would stand behind the respondent. The very short time given to her to respond to CLS's solicitors' letter of 30 August 2011, which must have taken much longer to prepare, and the manner of its service on her, were similarly inappropriate. Furthermore, CLS had not properly verified the only serious allegation of impropriety made by it against the respondent, namely that she had surreptitiously invited managers from Klarius/QH to a rugby match at Twickenham sponsored by CLS, thus demonstrating the closeness of her relationship with Klarius/QH even while she was an employee of CLS. Before the judge, it was common ground that the evidence of CLS was false, having been demonstrated to be so by the respondent."

8.3.2   Having refused the application for an injunction, the Court awarded indemnity costs against the claimant.

8.3.3   In *IFQT Services v Sherry* (QB, unreported November 2013), a disproportionate and aggressively pursued application was dismissed with indemnity costs. The defendant was a sales manager for a company which sold and resold tickets for sporting events. He had 12-month PTRs and, only on the expiry of 12 months, had got a job with a competing business. The claimant alleged he had taken customer lists and other documents and was inevitably using them. It asked the defendant, unsuccessfully, to agree to have his computers examined and to give undertakings not to contact customers. Proceedings were commenced and the claimant threatened to apply for an injunction but did not do so. The defendant provided a disclosure report showing that (limited) information had been emailed to his personal email from work. At that point the claimant applied for urgent interim relief consisting of disclosure of its documents in his possession, a witness statement explaining the use he made of the documents and an injunction

restraining him from making use of its confidential information.

8.3.4 The Judge said the claimant had adopted "an extreme approach,
       bullying and hectoring and asking for undertakings to which
       they were not entitled". The defendant had asked for evidence
       of breach which was not supplied. The conduct complained of
       was historic and there was no real threat against the claimant's
       interests.

8.4   *Recent cases*

8.4.1 Nevertheless, some of the more recent cases have suggested a
       judicial reluctance to award indemnity costs, and there is no
       doubt that they will be reserved for the more extreme cases.
       Two examples of this approach are given below.

8.4.2 In *Argus Media v Halim* [2019] EWHC 215 (QB), the claimant
       company was a price reporting agency. The defendant was a
       Business Development Manager in the claimant's fertiliser
       business. The claimant alleged that the defendant formed a
       price reporting agency named Afriqom to compete with its
       business in breach of the express and implied terms of his con-
       tract, by misusing the claimant's confidential information and
       in breach of non-solicitation and non-dealing covenants. The
       claimant sought indemnity costs relying on the defendant's
       unreasonable conduct. Amongst other things, they relied on the
       following facts: (1) before the claimant made the application, in
       response to requests for information the defendant had failed to
       provide "a full or accurate account of his plans" and "such
       information as he did provide was misleading"; (2) the
       defendant had concealed information relating to his intended
       business; and (3) the Judge had observed that the defendant's
       disclosure had been "wholly inadequate". However, although
       the defendant's conduct was found to be "regrettable", an order
       for indemnity costs was not justified because his conduct was
       not "outside the norm" (the test in *Excelsior Commercial &*

Industrial Holdings Ltd v Salisbury Hammer Aspden & Johnson [2002] EWCA Civ 879).

8.4.3   In *Praxis Capital Ltd v Burgess* [2015] EWHC 1801 (Ch), the Court had to determine the appropriate costs order following the claimant employer's unsuccessful action to enforce PTRs against the defendant who worked as an investment manager. The defendant sought indemnity costs on the basis that: (1) the judge had observed that the litigation had been prosecuted almost to the point of persecution by the claimant; (2) the claimant had exaggerated its evidence and its witnesses had failed to concede obvious points; and (3) the claimant's aim in bringing the action was not to protect its legitimate business interests, but to hound a former employee. The Judge concluded that it would not be appropriate to order costs on the indemnity basis. Rather, it was "indeed hard-fought commercial litigation by parties who [...] certainly did not get on with each other". Further, it was relevant that to some extent the defendant had contributed to the initiation of the litigation by copying the confidential information from his work laptop, which he had not been entitled to do.

8.5   Breach of an injunction – Committal

8.5.1   Committal of a person to prison for breach of an order is a serious matter and is exceptional. Under CPR rule 84.1, the power to commit exists for both failing to comply with an order and failing to comply with an undertaking. However, a recent case has served as a reminder that even in an employee competition case a defendant's conduct in breaching a court order may be enough to justify committal to prison.

8.5.2   In *OCS Group v Jagdeep Dadi* [2017] EWHC 1727 (Ch) the employer had lost a contract to a competitor. It brought a claim against the defendants alleging that they had committed breaches of their employment contracts, fiduciary duties and duties of confidence by transmitting confidential information to their home email addresses and then transmitting that information to a competitor. The interlocutory injunction, which contained a penal notice, prevented the employee from disclosing the employer's confidential information and required him to preserve hard copy and electronic documents and not to disclose the existence of the order to anyone. The employee admitted that he had deleted emails which could not be retrieved and had told the competitor about the order. The employer applied for committal to prison for the breaches.

8.5.3   The Court imposed a "short sentence" of six weeks in prison to mark its strong disapproval and to act as a deterrent in relation to his further compliance and as a warning to others who might be tempted to flout the court's orders. The contempts were deliberate and contumacious breaches. They had significantly prejudiced the employer and put them to considerable cost in forensic examination to salvage information which should have been left intact. The Court had accepted his apology was sincere and took account of his good character and the effect on his family.

CHAPTER NINE
CONFIDENTIAL INFORMATION – HOW IS IT DEFINED AND HOW CAN IT BE PROTECTED?

9.0.1. Cases involving actual or threatened competition by employees often involve the misuse of the employer's confidential information. There is therefore an important crossover between employee competition law and the law relating to the protection of confidential information. A claim for breach of confidence can be based on equitable obligations, independently of any express or implied terms of the contract. Claims will often be founded on breach of contract and simultaneously based on breach of equitable obligations. Breach of confidence is most likely to be relevant in an employee competition scenario as a basis to seek an injunction preventing the misuse of confidential information. The retention or misuse of confidential information can also be a basis for different types of interim relief including:

(i) delivery up of the confidential information;

(ii) orders permitting searches to be made of defendants' computer systems for information retained;

(iii) doorstep orders;

(iv) in an appropriate case, search and seizure orders permitting entry onto defendants' premises in order to identify and remove confidential information which has been taken inappropriately.

9.0.2. These orders are considered in detail in Chapter 10 below.

9.1.   The legal basis for using breach of confidence in employee competition cases

9.1.1   For the purposes of a breach of confidence action, in order to qualify as confidential, information must comply with the following three conditions (per *Coco v A N Clark (Engineers) Newspapers Ltd* [1969] RPC 41):

    i   it must have the necessary quality of confidence;

    ii   it must have been imparted in circumstances importing an obligation of confidence;

    iii there must have been unauthorised use of the confidential information to the detriment of the person entitled to the benefit of the information.

9.1.2   The first requirement, the "quality of confidence", requires that the information is inaccessible: it cannot be common knowledge or generally in the public domain. Whether it is generally accessible is a matter of fact and degree. Even if it is known by a small number of competing firms, if it is not generally available it will still have the necessary quality of confidence.

9.1.3   In *Trailfinders v Travel Counsellors Ltd* [2020] IRLR 448, the two defendants took a significant amount of client contact information and provided it to their new employer. They argued that it was not confidential as it was available from public sources. The Court held that it was no defence to a breach of confidence action based on the taking of confidential data that the information could have been obtained from publicly available sources. The identity of the clients was not generally known. It was also no defence that the information was also part of one of the employee's experience and skills, held within his memory. The Court would not accept an argument that the employee went to the trouble of copying information although he need not have bothered because it was in his mind: the information went beyond his experience and skills, at least in part, and the copying was done in breach of the implied terms of his contract.

9.1.4   As to the second requirement, the test as to whether this is satisfied appears to be based on what the employee ought to have appreciated; in essence a test of actual *or* constructive knowledge which is objective rather than subjective. This is the position confirmed by *Primary Group (UK) Ltd v RBS* [2014] EWHC 1082 (Ch), para 222, which considered conflicting statements which had been made by Lord Neuberger PSC in *Vestergaard Frandsen A/S v Bestnet Europe Ltd* [2013] IRLR 654 (SC) as to whether it was a test of actual or constructive knowledge. Further confirmation that the test is what the defendant knew or ought to have known was recently given in *Trailfinders Ltd v Travel Counsellors Ltd* [2020] IRLR 448 at para 42.

9.1.5   The third requirement in *Coco* may need to be qualified in cases where an employee has taken information but not done anything with it. Where an injunction is sought, the element of detrimental breach is controversial. An example is *Brandeaux v Chadwick* [2011] IRLR 224 in which the High Court considered the position of Ms Chadwick who, in the course of her employment, had sent a "huge number" of confidential documents relating to her employer's affairs to her personal email account. Her purpose was to arm herself for the future in any disputes with Brandeaux by being able to report matters to the regulators. Other than that, she had no intention to misuse the information for her own benefit or to their detriment. The Judge held that transferring the information amounted to a breach of the duty of fidelity and as it remained confidential to her employer, they were entitled in principle to its return. However, as the employer had the information the Judge held that the appropriate order was for the destruction of the employer's material on her hard drive. There were no damages because the employer had suffered no loss. Subsequent cases have looked in more detail into the availability of damages in cases where confidential information has been wrongfully taken, but not used. These are considered further in Chapter 13.

9.2   Types of confidential information

9.2.1   There are three classes of confidential information (per *Faccenda Chicken v Fowler* [1986] ICR 297):

i   Information too trivial to be protectable

ii   Information protectable without covenant but only during the currency of employment

iii   Information which is a trade secret and protectable without covenant after the employment has ended. This category includes information which, whilst not properly described as a trade secret, is of such a highly confidential nature as to require the same protection.

9.2.2   Importantly, subsequent cases have recognised that the third category includes customer contact details and other customer information.

9.2.3   In *Lansing Linde Ltd v Kerr* [1991] ICR 428 (CA), the Court of Appeal held that a trade secret is information which, if disclosed to a competitor, would be liable to cause real (or significant) harm to the owner of the secret. It must be information used in a trade or business, and secondly the owner must limit the dissemination of it or at least not encourage or permit widespread publication. The Court recognised that this may include the identities of customers and the goods which they buy.

9.2.4   In *FSS Travel & Leisure* [1998] IRLR 385, the Court of Appeal stated, at para 34, that lists of customer names and addresses and the private information of customers are protectable without covenant during the currency of employment and their removal and/or misuse is a breach of contract. They said that in addressing the question of whether it is a trade secret, the court needed to examine the nature of the employment, the character of the information, the restrictions imposed on its dissemination, the extent of its use in the public domain and the damage likely to be caused by its disclosure.

9.2.5 *Printers & Finishers v Holloway* [1965] 1 WLR 1 provided another useful touchstone: whether a man of average intelligence and honesty would think there was anything improper in putting his memory of the matters in question at the disposal of his new employers.

9.2.6 Relevant factors in deciding whether the information is a trade secret include the nature of the information, the nature of the employment and any emphasis placed by the employer on confidentiality. Clearly the second part of the test in *Coco* above is relevant here: namely whether the information was "imparted in circumstances importing an obligation of confidence".

9.3. <u>The Trade Secrets (Enforcement, etc.) Regulations 2018:</u>
<u>basic provisions</u>

9.3.1 On 9 June 2018 the UK brought into force the Trade Secrets (Enforcement, etc.) Regulations 2018 ("the Regulations") in order to implement the EU Trade Secrets Directive ("the Directive"), the purpose of which was to address the uneven protections of trade secrets in EU Member States by bringing legal clarity and establishing a level playing field between all European companies. The provisions of the Regulations are set out below only by way of a summary.

9.3.2 Regulation 3(1) creates a statutory tort:

> *"The acquisition, use or disclosure of a trade secret is unlawful where the acquisition, use or disclosure constitutes a breach of confidence in confidential information."*

9.3.3   Trade secrets are defined under the Regulations (r.2) as any information which

     i   is secret, in the sense that it is not, as a body, or in the precise configuration of its components, generally known among or readily accessible to, persons within the circles that normally deal with the kind of information in question,

     ii   has commercial value because it is secret, and

     iii has been subject to reasonable steps to keep it secret.

9.3.4   The Regulations create statutory causes of action for the misuse of confidential information, for which the limitation period in England and Wales is six years. In Scotland the prescriptive period is five years (r.4-5).

9.3.5   There is provision for a number of measures which a court may take to preserve confidentiality of trade secrets in the course of proceedings, such as limiting access to hearings and to documents referring to trade secrets and providing a redacted version of any judicial decision (r. 10 and 18).

9.3.6   Regulations 11 to 15 provide for the court to take various interim and final measures, including the prohibition of the use or disclosure of the trade secret, the seizure or delivery up of infringing goods and the destruction of an electronic file containing the trade secret.

9.3.7   Regulation 16 provides that a court may order compensation in lieu of an injunction or may order corrective measures under Regulation 14.

9.3.8   By Regulation 17, a court must order someone who knew or ought to have known they had infringed the Regulations to pay the secret holder damages appropriate to the actual prejudice suffered as a result of the acquisition, use or disclosure. A court may award damages either

i   on a part economic basis (taking account of lost profits, and of any unfair profits made by the infringer) and part non-economic basis (including taking account of the moral prejudice caused to the trade secret holder by the unlawful acquisition, use or disclosure);

ii   or, where appropriate, on the basis of the royalties or fees that would have been available had the infringer obtained a licence to use the trade secret in question.

9.3.9   Regulation 19 sets out the proceedings to which the regulations apply, namely those

- Brought before a court after the coming into force of the Regulations

- In respect of a claim for unlawful acquisition, use or disclosure of a trade secret

- For the application of measures, procedures and remedies provided for under the Regulations.

9.4   The Trade Secrets (Enforcement, etc.) Regulations 2018: inter-relation with common law and equitable breach of confidence

9.4.1   The relationship between the Regulations and the concept of breach of confidence and misuse of confidential information in common law and equity has caused considerable debate and has yet to be fully worked out by the courts. It is also possible that the significance of the Regulations, assuming they remain in force, will be watered down following the departure of the UK from the European Union.

9.4.2   The Regulations themselves attempt to clarify this relationship by Regulation 3, which provides:

> *(2) A trade secret holder may apply for and a court may grant measures, procedures, and remedies available in an action for breach of confidence where the measures, procedures and remedies—*
>
> > *(a) provide wider protection to the trade secret holder than that provided under these Regulations in respect of the unlawful acquisition, use or disclosure of a trade secret, and*
> >
> > *(b) comply with the safeguards referred to in Article 1 of [the Trade Secrets Directive].*
>
> *(3) A trade secret holder may apply for and a court may grant the measures, procedures and remedies referred to in paragraph (2) in addition, or as an alternative, to the measures, procedures and remedies provided for in these Regulations in respect of the unlawful acquisition, use or disclosure of a trade secret.*

9.4.3   The safeguards referred to in Article 1 of the Directive include that the Directive shall not affect the right to freedom of expression nor offer any ground for restricting the mobility of employees through the use of their experience and skills honestly acquired in the normal course of their employment.

9.4.4   The obvious interpretation of these provisions is that the Regulations provide a statutory cause of action for breach of confidence, and remedies, which can run alongside, or in addition to, claims for breach of confidence under the existing law. There may be an argument that under Regulation 3(2) above, an equitable breach of confidence action could only be brought to the extent it gives wider protection than that under the Regulations, although the Regulations are silent as to the position in respect of common law claims. In any event, it is likely that for the time being at least, proceedings that are brought for breach of confidence or misuse of trade secrets will be accompanied by a claim under the Regulations.

9.4.5 At the time of publication, one reported case has referred to the inter-relationship between English law and the Directive/Regulations: *Trailfinders Ltd v Travel Counsellors Ltd* [2020] IRLR 448, the facts of which are set out above at paragraph 9.1.3. Hacon J observed that the implementation of the Directive through the Regulations did not involve any change in the law. He further observed that the explanatory note to the Regulations stated that a number of provisions of the Directive had been implemented in the UK by the principles of common law and equity and by statute and court rules and concluded that it was to be "assumed that the substantive principles governing the protection of confidential information under English law, including that afforded by terms implied into contracts of employment and by equitable obligations of confidence, are unaffected by the Trade Secrets Directive", although "the Directive shines an occasional light on those principles" [original emphasis]. He went on to hold that the copying of the information breached both common law and equitable obligations and was an unlawful act under the Directive.

9.5 LinkedIn access and contacts as confidential information

9.5.1 Employers often seek to prevent employees taking away their contacts on LinkedIn and access to corporate LinkedIn groups after leaving their employment. Whilst the analysis below focuses on LinkedIn, the principles below also apply to other social media platforms.

9.5.2 The question of whether a LinkedIn profile and/or contacts fall within the category of confidential information which an employer can protect by an injunction depends on the circumstances. The crucial question in most cases is who owns the asset. If the employer is shown to have a proprietary interest in it, they are likely to be able to get delivery up and other forms of interim relief. If the asset contains trade secrets, or the employer's confidential information such as customer contact details, then it is all the more protectable.

9.5.3 There are various measures the employer can take to help to ensure the information is protectable, such as inserting clauses at the beginning of the employment making it clear who owns the cloud-based platform and the account. A clause asserting a proprietary interest in such an account which is set up after the individual has started in the employment could be effective notwithstanding that it has been set up in the name of the individual employee. Such an account might, for example, be used by an employee to market the services which the employer provides, and to seek new contacts for whom they can offer the employer's services. More difficult issues are likely to arise where an employee brings their own LinkedIn profile to a new employment. A clause seeking to restrict the retention and use of that profile after departure might face challenge on the basis that it is not protecting a legitimate interest of the employer. However, a clause giving the employer a proprietary right in client contact information added to a LinkedIn profile during employment is more likely to be effective.

9.5.4 In an appropriate case, the court may grant interim relief on a springboard basis to return control of corporate LinkedIn 'groups' to the employee's former employer: *Whitmar Publications v Gamage* [2013] EWHC 1881 (Ch). The claimant in that case had managed these groups as part of her employment and the groups had been used as a source of email addresses for marketing for the employee's new business.

9.5.5 It is long established that it is unlawful to appropriate a compilation of customer contacts for the purposes of future competition through LinkedIn: see *Hays Specialist Recruitment (Holdings) v Ions* [2008] IRLR 904, involving transferring contacts to LinkedIn with a view to the subsequent use of that information in a competing business.

9.6 <u>Human Rights Act defences to actions based on disclosure of confidential information</u>

9.6.1 Since the enactment of the Human Rights Act 1998 ("HRA"), the impact of Convention rights on claims relating to the misuse of confidential information must always be considered. Whilst the impact of the HRA on breach of confidence actions relating to the unauthorised disclosure of personal information is significant, its impact on the courts' approach to commercially confidential information has been more limited. It will therefore be dealt with here only by way of overview. Nevertheless, points about Convention rights have been taken in a number of recent cases and it is important to be aware of when such issues might arise.

9.6.2 The law in this area has developed by reference to the right of privacy conferred by Article 8 of the European Convention on Human Rights and has required a balancing of that right against the right to freedom of expression conferred by Article 10. In practice this means that the court might decline to prohibit the disclosure of information where that might affect a party's freedom of expression. This is most likely to arise on an interim application for injunctive relief. Section 12 HRA expressly applies if a court is considering whether to grant any relief which might affect freedom of expression. Section 12(3) and (4) of the HRA are particularly relevant in this situation. Section 12(3) provides:

> "*No such relief which might affect the exercise of the Convention right to freedom of expression is to be granted so as to restrain publication before trial unless the court is satisfied that the applicant is likely to establish that publication should not be allowed.*"

9.6.3   Section 12(4) provides that the court must have particular regard to the importance of the Convention right to freedom of expression. Where the relevant material appears to be literary, journalistic or artistic, the court must have regard to the extent to which (i) the material has, or is about to, become available to the public, and (ii) it is in the public interest for the material to be published.

9.6.4   The threshold test when applying for an interim injunction is derived from *American Cyanamid Co v Ethicon Ltd* [1975] AC 396 and requires that the party applying for an injunction shows that there is a 'serious issue to be tried'. However, the cases establish that where the right to freedom of expression is engaged, the applicant must get over a higher hurdle, in that the court should not restrain disclosure unless it is satisfied that the applicant's prospects of success at trial are sufficiently favourable to justify such an order being made in the particular circumstances of the case. Hence the claimant would ordinarily be required by the court to satisfy it that s/he would be more likely than not to succeed at trial. This is a higher threshold than the 'serious issue' test and is often referred to as the 'enhanced merits test'.

9.6.5   The enhanced merits test was confirmed in the leading case of *Cream Holdings v Banerjee* [2005] 1 AC 253 (HL) (see para 22). The claimants were attempting to restrain publication of confidential information concerning alleged financial irregularities which a former employee had supplied to a local newspaper. The House of Lords discharged an injunction which had been granted by the Judge, having concluded that the disclosures were matters of significant public interest and that therefore the right to freedom of expression was engaged.

9.6.6   The fact that the dispute may be a commercial one does not of itself mean that S12(3) is inapplicable, as stated by Longmore LJ at *Boehringer Ingelheim v Vetplus Ltd* [2007] BusLR 1456 para 55. However, the recent cases are helpful in demonstrating that dissemination to a small number of parties in furtherance of a defendant's financial interests is relatively unlikely to engage any Convention rights.

9.6.7 In *Awbury Technical Solutions Llc v Karson Management (Bermuda)* [2019] EWHC 233 (Comm), a case which concerned businesses providing finance for collateral loan obligations, the Court's response to an argument that Convention rights were engaged was to focus on the absence of anything that could be described as publication. The defendant was introduced to the claimant by a reinsurer as a potential funder for a particular transaction. As a result the defendant was given details of the claimant's business and intended structures and pricing, but the information was protected by a 'non-disclosure agreement'. The defendant then disclosed this confidential information to other reinsurers to assist it in developing its own business.

9.6.8 The issue was whether the right to freedom of expression was engaged by the defendant using the information about the claimant's finance scheme in implementing its own scheme, which involved communicating it to potential participants in confidence. The Judge, Butcher J, said that "where communication is made only for the purposes of furthering the financial interests of the communicator to a very limited range of other individuals whose interest in it is simply to further their financial interests, and where there is no question of the information which is imparted being of a journalistic, literary or artistic nature I consider that it will not, some extraordinary feature apart, involve the right to freedom of expression" (para 35). He contrasted this with communication to the press, and some forms of advertising, which could be classed as commercial, but which could nevertheless engage the right.

9.6.9 As a result, he concluded that the right was not engaged and the *American Cyanamid* test applied, rather than the enhanced merits test.

9.6.10 *Awbury* can be contrasted with the more recent case of *Pharmagona Ltd v Taheri* [2020] EWHC 312 (QB) in which Nicol J was dealing with an injunction to restrain former employees of the pharmaceutical company – a husband and wife – from using confidential information they had taken. The defendants alleged that the claimant had been engaged in criminal activities, including exports to Iran in an improper manner, and as they feared they would not be believed, they had downloaded the relevant evidence. They had already disclosed some matters to the Civil Aviation Authority, which had led to an investigation.

9.6.11 Nicol J considered, albeit without much analysis of the point, that on these facts, this was a case to which the test in section 12(3) HRA applied (relief could not be granted unless the court was satisfied that the applicant was likely to establish at trial that publication should not be allowed) rather than the lower test in *American Cyanamid*. Nevertheless, he still felt able to grant an interim injunction because he considered the claimant was likely to succeed at trial in showing that the defendants would be likely to make use of its confidential information. The injunction prevented disclosure to the world at large, but in an unusual twist, he said that they should be free to continue to cooperate with the Civil Aviation Authority or any other public authority and the injunction should contain a proviso that would allow them to answer questions from such authorities or provide documents which those authorities requested. He refused to make an order for delivery up of the documents for the same reason.

9.6.12 In conclusion, the position in relation to HRA defences can be summarised as follows. In cases involving the dissemination of information by a departing employee to a new employer, or to a very limited category of people, the Article 10 right to freedom of expression, and the merits test under s.12(3) HRA are unlikely to be engaged unless there are exceptional features. However, even in a commercial context the Convention right might be engaged in a case involving communication to the press, certain forms of advertising to the public or disclosure in good faith to a regulatory body.

CHAPTER TEN
WHAT TO DO IF THERE ARE NO CONTRACTUAL RESTRAINTS ON SOLICITING AND COMPETING

Springboard injunctions, garden leave, affirming the contract and the Databases Regulations

10.0.1. It is often the case that an employee's employment contract does not contain any PTRs at all; or, indeed, he/she may not even have a written contract of employment. If an employee takes steps to compete whilst still employed or removes confidential information (eg customer lists and pricing), the employer still has significant remedies available to it.

10.0.2. In the absence of effective express covenants, in order to protect its interests, an employer could rely upon:-

a) the implied obligation of fidelity – but this will come to an end with the termination of the employment relationship;

b) fiduciary duties, where they exist – these will generally come to an end with the end of the relationship or obligation giving rise to the duty but there are some exceptions;

c) equitable duties of confidentiality – after employment ends, absent any wrongdoing whilst employed, these are likely to assist only in respect of trade secrets or information of that same level of confidentiality; the enforcement of these duties is now supported by the Trade Secrets (Enforcement, etc.) Regulations 2018, which are discussed in Chapter 9;

    d)   the Copyright and Rights in Databases Regulations 1997 – these are often relevant where information in the form of lists has been removed prior to the employment ending;

    e)   breach of Directors' duties under the Companies Act 2006.

10.0.3. Assuming the employee has left, in these circumstances most claims will be based on the following assertions:

    (a) that the employee unlawfully competed or prepared to compete whilst still employed and that has given him/her an unfair advantage in the new business after leaving and/or caused financial damage; and/or

    (b) that the employee unlawfully took or removed confidential information belonging to the employer, whilst still employed or subsequently, which they have used to gain an advantage or have given to a competitor.

10.1.   Fiduciary duties

10.1.1. It is the duty to act selflessly, in the interests of the principal, which distinguishes a fiduciary from someone who merely owes contractual obligations. This extends to not making an unauthorised profit; not putting him or herself in a position where his duty and interest conflict; and not acting for his own benefit without the informed consent of the principal (per *Sinclair Investments v Versailles Trade Finance* [2012] Ch 453, Lord Neuburger).

10.1.2. The fiduciary duties owed by company directors are reflected in the general duties for directors set out in the Companies Act 2006. These are considered in the next section.

10.1.3. It is well known that company directors owe fiduciary duties by virtue of their positions, but other employees may also do so. In *Ranson v Customer Systems* [2012] IRLR 769, the Court of Appeal warned that it was dangerous to reason by analogy from cases about company directors to cases about employees when determining the scope of fiduciary obligations (see para 24 ibid.). A fiduciary duty does not arise by virtue of the position or job title; rather it is necessary to identify the particular duties performed by the employee and to ask whether in all the circumstances he has placed himself in a position where he must act solely in the interest of his employer.

10.1.4. The extent to which fiduciary duties other than those of company directors survive the termination of employment is a matter of ongoing debate in the case law. However, in relation to directors, some of the statutory duties do survive. Section 170(2) Companies Act 2006 states that someone who ceases to be a director continues to be subject to the duty to avoid conflicts of interest (s.175) as regards the exploitation of any property, information or opportunity of which he became aware when a director and the duty not to accept benefits from third parties (s.176) in respect of things done or omitted before he ceased to be a director.

10.2. Directors' duties

10.2.1. It is worth noting that alongside their fiduciary duties, company directors owe a number of duties under statute, which are expressly stated to be based on common law and equitable principles (see s.170(3) Companies Act 2006). These provisions of the Companies Act 2006 apply to those in the position of a director, including a de facto director. It is emphasised that these statutory duties do not apply to other employees or to partners or members of an LLP. Breaches of these duties are sometimes pleaded in addition to fiduciary duties in employee competition claims. The key duties in the Companies Act 2006 are:

i   Section 171: to act within their powers;

ii   Section 172: to act in good faith and promote the interests of the company;

iii Section 173: to exercise independent judgment;

iv Section 174: to exercise reasonable care, skill and judgment;

v   Section 175: the duty to avoid conflicts of interest;

vi Section 176: the duty not to accept benefits from third parties;

vii Section 177 (and 182-187): the duty to declare an interest in a proposed or existing transaction or arrangement.

10.2.2.   Whilst it is advisable for an employer to refer to breaches of these obligations in any claim where they are relevant, they may not add anything of substance to allegations of breach of fidelity and fiduciary duties because under section 178, "the consequences of breach (or threatened breach) of sections 171 to 177 are the same as would apply if the corresponding common law rule or equitable principle applied"[1].

10.3.   The implied obligation of fidelity

10.3.1.   Every contract of employment contains an implied term that the employee will render faithful service to the employer. An employee will be in breach of this term if he/she does anything which will damage his/her employer's business or, potentially, if he/she renders services to anyone else during the period of employment.

---

1 Although note that under s.177, in the event the company enters into the impugned transaction, the director is under a new and continuing duty to disclose, expressed in substantially similar terms, in s.182. Breach of that, separate, duty is a criminal offence under s.183.

10.3.2. The basic obligation is to be loyal to his/her employer and to act in his/her employer's best interests. The employee must act in good faith and must receive and obey the employer's instructions and devote his or her time and talents to his employer's business: *Helmet v Tunnard* [2007] IRLR 126, para 26.

10.4. <u>What is the difference between the duty of fidelity and fiduciary duties?</u>

10.4.1. Breach of fiduciary duty gives rise to an equitable remedy whereas the duty of fidelity is contractual. Whereas equity will generally require any profits to be paid over as the best means of protecting the beneficiary, the common law will only award the victim of a breach of contract what he or she expected to gain from the arrangement.

10.4.2. The key feature of the obligation of a fiduciary is that the employee owes a duty to act solely in the interests of his employer and not in his own interests: see the distinction in case of *University of Nottingham v Fishel* [2000] IRLR 471.

10.4.3. Unlike the fiduciary, the employee is entitled to pursue his/her own self interest, save where prevented from doing so by the contract. This difference is well illustrated by *Helmet Integrated Systems v Tunnard* [2007] IRLR 126.

10.4.4. Helmet Integrated Systems produced and sold protective equipment, including helmets of the sort used by the London Fire Brigade. The defendant was a senior salesman with an idea for a new type of helmet. He took various steps (in his free time) to develop his idea, and to set up a business to market and sell it. He then resigned and began in business through a newly incorporated company.

10.4.5. The case was concerned with whether the steps he took whilst still an employee breached any obligations to his employer.

The defendant had not been a director, merely an employee. The main battle ground was whether or not there was a fiduciary obligation which Helmet could point to as having been broken. The defendant's contract of employment had contained the following terms:

(i) to "act at all times with the best interests of the company in mind…"

(ii) to "advise on competitor activity and pricing structures"

(iii) and that "no employee will be permitted to undertake any work or arrange the undertaking of any work which can be seen to affect adversely or be in competition with the company".

10.4.6. The Court of Appeal in *Helmet*

(i) usefully emphasised that there is no clear line between legitimate pre-termination activity and illegitimate activity, and that we should not be beguiled into thinking that because an activity is preparatory that it is permitted. What is permitted will continue to depend on facts of the individual case;

(ii) were prepared to accept that the effect of the terms above was that the defendant owed an obligation as a fiduciary not to misuse information about the activity of competitors for the benefit of himself or someone other than Helmet;

(iii) but declined to find him in breach of any contractual or fiduciary duty. The basis was twofold. Firstly, they spoke of the right to prepare to compete as a positive right rather than a residual right, and in that context took the view that "Clear words are needed to restrict the ordinary freedom of an employee who is considering quitting his employment and setting up in competition to his former employer". Secondly, they found that any fiduciary duty arising out of the terms and circumstances of the contract was not wide enough to require him to report his own activities.

10.4.7. In *Ranson v Customer Systems* [2012] IRLR 769 the Court of Appeal gave further guidance on the scope of both fiduciary duties and the duty of fidelity. The defendant worked in a sales function for the employer, which provided specialist information technology consultancy. He was not a director but had direct or indirect responsibility for a significant part of their revenue. He resigned, and before and during his notice period he made preparations to establish a business in competition. Two days before his employment terminated an order was placed, due to him discussing potential work with clients. The Court found that he did not owe fiduciary duties and the placing of an order was not a breach of fidelity as it was not the diversion of a business opportunity which might have gone to the defendant.

10.4.8. The Court of Appeal's reasoning in *Ranson* was as follows:

i   Unlike directorships, not every employment contract gives rise to fiduciary relationships.

ii   As the nature of fiduciary obligations will vary depending on the relationship, it is dangerous to reason by analogy from cases about directors to cases about employees. The first question is always whether fiduciary obligations arise at all and that is entirely dependent on the contract.

iii The duty of loyalty or fidelity, as set out in *University of Nottingham v Fishel* [2000] IRLR 471, requires each party to have regard to the interests of the other, but not that either must subjugate his or her own interests to those of the other.

iv   Further, *Fishel* confirmed there was no general principle that an employee must inform his employer if and when he is doing outside work in breach of his contract.

v   Whilst it was possible that such a disclosure obligation could arise out of an employment contract, it did not in this case. *Helmet Integrated Systems Ltd v Tunnard* suggested that where an employee learned information about the activities of a competitor, the misuse of which rendered the employer vulnerable, fiduciary obligations might arise. This was not the situation in the present case as the defendant did not divert or interfere with any business opportunity being pursued by his employer and the claimant continued to deal with the client who had placed an order.

vi   The argument that *Item Software v Fassihi* [2004] EWCA Civ 1244 had altered the position such that a disclosure obligation existed for all employees was rejected.

vii   The implied term of trust and confidence could not be used to create fiduciary obligations, as it does not impose a positive duty and is conceptually different, being a matter of contract law, not of the law of fiduciary obligations.

10.4.9.   *Re-Use Collections v Sendall* [2015] IRLR 226 provides a recent example of a case where despite being very senior, the employee did not owe fiduciary duties. The defendant was a senior employee of the claimant glass recycling business. He had formerly owned the business before it had been bought by the claimant's operation. Six months prior to his departure he set up a company ("Newco") in which he intended to compete with Re-Use, together with his sons. By two months prior, he was actively contacting the claimant's suppliers and at least one of their customers with a view to winning their business for his new company. He was spending by then a significant amount of his time whilst at work on matters relating to Newco. He gave three months' notice of termination and shortly afterwards the claimant discovered what he was doing and suspended him pending a disciplinary hearing relating to this conduct. He did not participate and they deemed that he had either resigned or been dismissed.

10.4.10.　The Court found he did not owe a fiduciary duty; one could not be inferred from the terms of his contract, nor from wider factors relied on by the claimant. He was a highly trusted, well-remunerated and long-standing senior employee and was in charge of the claimant's entire operation at Dagenham. But he was not a director and did not attend or even report to board meetings. There was no evidence he had any high-level responsibility: strategic, financial or otherwise (applying *Ranson v Customer Systems*).

10.4.11.　His actions did amount to a breach of the duty of fidelity. The Judge said this would be the case even if his conduct had been limited to providing finance for his two sons to set up the business (given that Newco was intended to be directly competitive, operating in the same area of the country and competing for the same pool of suppliers and customers, he could not have had that financial interest and carried out his duties fully). The defendant, his son and the company he had set up were liable for the tort of conspiracy to cause economic loss. However, on the particular facts of this case, the company he had set up could not be liable for inducing breach of contract.

10.5.　<u>When is preparing to compete unlawful as a breach of fidelity or fiduciary duties?</u>

Competition and fidelity

10.5.1.　As *Helmet* demonstrates, the employee is entitled to prepare for future activities to some extent without breaching the duty. However, whether acts are preparatory or not does not of itself determine whether they amount to a breach of the obligation of fidelity. Neither does the fact that the relevant activities are "reasonable or necessary" preparatory acts mean that the duty of fidelity has not been breached: *Helmet* para 51. However, *Helmet* has given rise to controversy and is seen as a case which gives considerable latitude to middle-ranking employees, albeit the defendant in that case was not seen as dishonest and acted alone, without involving other employees.

10.5.2. Some points taken from other cases may assist to clarify where the line is drawn:

   i In *Lancashire Fires v Lyons* [1997] IRLR 113 the employee's actions-- buying equipment and renting premises-- had fallen *well* on the wrong side of the line. But note that the employee here had misused confidential information for the purposes of his business: the duty of good faith may demand higher standards of loyalty where the employee has access to confidential information and different types of job engage different degrees of fidelity (ibid. paras 20, 49 and 51).

   ii In *Balston v Headline Filters* [1990] FSR 385 the following acts by a director were found to be permissible whilst employed:

   a entering into a lease for a commercial premises;

   b purchasing an off-shelf company;

   c investigating the possibility of setting up in competition including consulting accountants, solicitors and his bank.

   The following were found to breach the duty of fidelity:

a   telling a customer that he was leaving and would soon be in a position to supply product (which led to an order being placed);

b   recruiting one of the claimant's employees.

iii   In *British Midland Tool v Midland International Tooling* [2003] 2 BCLC 523 three remaining directors were aware that another director, who had resigned and who they planned to join, had made a determined attempt to poach the existing workforce. Hart J considered that it was impossible to hold that the conduct was consistent with their duty of fidelity to their employer.

iv   The courts have found that it does not follow from the fact that a company did not trade until the employee's contract was terminated that the employee's ability to serve the employers was unimpaired while the contract persisted. It may cause the employee difficulties serving the employer faithfully and honestly: *Shepherd's Investments v Walters* [2007] IRLR 110, para 131.

v   In *Reuse Collections*, actively contacting the claimant's suppliers and at least one of their customers with a view to winning their business was found to breach the duty and the Judge said there would have been a breach even if all he had done was provide finance for his two sons to set up a competing business.

vi   In *Gamatronic (UK) Ltd v Hamilton & Mansfield* [2017] BCC 670, two directors (H and M) were found to be in breach of their duties of fidelity and fiduciary duties in actions they took prior to leaving to join a competitor. However, the employers were not ultimately entitled to a remedy. The defendants were directors and employees of, and shareholders in, the first claimant UK company (G), which they had established together with its parent company, the second claimant. It was alleged that they had secretly set up and held beneficial interests in a competing business (V) before they left G under compromise agreements. It was held that they owed fiduciary duties and duties of fidelity to avoid conflict of interest, to promote the success of the business and to disclose the nature of any interest they had in the competitor V.

vii The defendants in *Gamatronic* asserted they did not consider that V was competitive with G's business. The court found that it was and they should reasonably have come to that conclusion. The question of competition was to be determined objectively, not according to their subjective belief. During the latter period of their employment, H had helped set up V's price list and M had deliberately concealed the nature of a trip made to develop V's business. They had approached customers on V's behalf, holding themselves out as V's directors and being actively involved in V's operational matters.

viii In *Alesco Risk Management Services v Bishopsgate Insurance* [2019] EWHC 2839 (QB) it was stated that it will almost invariably be breach of fidelity if an employee (i) recruits/ encourages/ solicits other employees to leave the employer's employment, or (ii) assists another employer to recruit a colleague by providing information to the rival employer.

Competition and fiduciary

10.5.3.   In respect of fiduciary duties, some pointers from the case law will be the most useful guide as to when pre-termination competitive activity breaches the fiduciary duty and when it does not.

i   "[T]he essence of the obligation of an employee as fiduciary is that the employee must act solely or exclusively in the interest of his employer": *Helmet* para 33.

ii   When dealing with activity which is on the borderline of being impermissible, the courts may be more inclined to find a breach of the fidelity duty if the employee also has fiduciary obligations: *Helmet* para 33.

iii   In many cases fiduciary duties and the obligation of fidelity would draw the line between permissible preparation and unlawful acts in competition in a similar place. The two important points to emphasise here are as follows. First, as explained in *Ranson*, there is no fixed category of fiduciary obligations. The extent of them, if they exist, depends entirely on the nature of the job and the terms of the contracts. Second, there is nevertheless a fundamental obligation on a fiduciary to report wrongdoing or threats to the company, and this certainly applies to statutory directors under the Companies Act 2006. This is not necessarily part of the duty of fidelity as the cases above confirm.

iv   The law is keen to protect the rights of all employees, including directors, to prepare for future competition:

> Whilst "*the twin principles, that a director must act towards his company with honesty, good faith, and loyalty and must avoid any conflict of interest, are firmly in place, and are exacting requirements, exactingly enforced ... their application in different circumstances has required care and sensitivity both to the facts and to other principles, such as that of personal freedom to compete, where that does not intrude on the misuse of the company's property whether in the form of business opportunities or trade*

secrets": *Foster Bryant Surveying Ltd v Bryant* [2007] Bus LR 1565 (CA) at para 76 per Rix LJ.

v   In *Gamatronic*, in light of these principles, whilst parts of the defendants' activities did breach their fiduciary duties as described above, a significant part of their earlier preparatory activity did not (ibid. at para 147-149).

Conclusion

10.5.4.   Owing to the fact that the line between legitimate and illegitimate competition is so unclear, at the interim injunction stage it can be relatively easy to show that steps which are known to have been taken by an employee prior to leaving the business create a "serious question to be tried" about their activities.

10.6.   <u>Database rights</u>

10.6.1.   The Directive on the Legal Protection of Databases 96/9/EC ("the Database Directive") was given effect in English law by the Copyright and Rights in Databases Regulations 1997 (SI 1997/3032) ("the Regulations").

10.6.2.   The Regulations create a 'database right', which is a free-standing right distinct from both copyright and confidentiality and provides protection to the creator of a database.

10.6.3.   Database rights are infringed when a person extracts or re-utilises all or substantial parts of the contents of the database without the owner's consent. Extract means "the permanent or temporary transfer of those contents to another medium by any means or in any form" (reg 12(1)). Re-utilisation means making those contents available to the public by any means (reg 12(1)). To amount to an infringement, the extraction or re-utilisation must be of a substantial part of the database. Substantial means substantial in relation to quantity or quality or a combination of both (reg 12(1)).

10.6.4. Often, the argument centres around whether the material removed falls within the definition of a 'database', which is "a collection of independent works, data or other materials" which are

i   "arranged in a systematic or methodical way" and

ii   "individually accessible by electronic or other means." (reg 12(1))

10.6.5. It will be protected if "there has been a substantial investment in obtaining, verifying or presenting the contents of the database" (reg 13(1)) where investment is "any investment whether of financial, human or technical resources".

10.6.6. This is a broad definition and it is certainly possible that it would cover lists of contacts, and methodically arranged customer records on computer systems. However, other materials stored on computers are more marginal. For example, where correspondence and financial spreadsheets are concerned, depending on the facts it may be difficult to show that they were "arranged in a systematic or methodical way" and potentially even more difficult to show that there has been the "substantial investment" required by Regulation 13.

10.6.7. Where an employee takes a client list to a new employer, it is likely that the definition of extraction will be satisfied: see *Crowson Fabrics Ltd v Rider* [2008] IRLR 228 at para 119.

10.6.8. Remedies available for breach of database rights are those which are available for infringement of copyright under Ss96, 97 and 98 Copyright, Designs and Patents Act 1988: namely, damages, injunctions, accounts or otherwise.

Because the remedies are the same, claims based on database rights will not necessarily add anything to claims based on breaches of the duties of confidence and fidelity in removing the material, but there are some important differences:

i   there is no requirement that the information contained in the database is confidential; depending on the facts, this could be advantageous. As long as the material falls within the definition of a database and has been extracted or re-utilised, the statutory tort will be made out;

ii   in light of the definition of 'database' in the regulations, the evidence which would be needed to establish the definition will be different from that in any action relating to breach of confidence, as the focus is on investment in presenting the contents of the database, rather than on the quality of the contents themselves.

10.7.   Springboard Injunctions

10.7.1.   Competing with the employer or other action prejudicial to the employer's business whilst still employed will be a breach of the duty of fidelity and (if the employee is a fiduciary) a breach of fiduciary duty.

10.7.2.   There is also an implied term of confidentiality in every contract of employment so any removal of confidential information by an existing employee is also a breach of contract.

10.7.3.   Often the employer only becomes aware of the situation after (or just before) the employee has left to set up in competition. By the time s/he has left, in the absence of restrictive covenants, on the face of it there is no existing restriction on the employee's activities. The springboard injunction fills this gap by restricting the employee's activities after leaving in order to prevent them taking advantage of breaches of contract committed before the employment relationship ended and thereby obtaining a "springboard" advantage.

10.7.4.　　The basic principles are summarised in *QBE v Dymoke & Ors* [2012] IRLR 458. First, the form of the order and 'springboard' relief should fit the facts. Second, the 'springboard' relief should reflect and restrain the spectrum of the unlawful activities which made up the 'springboard'. Third, in granting 'springboard' relief, the court may restrain otherwise lawful activities taking place on unlawful foundations. Fourth, the form and content of the 'springboard' relief should match the tensile strength of the 'springboard' unlawfully used by a defendant. Fifth, in granting 'springboard' relief, the court should take account of all the circumstances and grant relief which it thinks is fair, just and equitable.

10.7.5.　　In *QBE v Dymoke*, Haddon-Cave J went on (at paras 240-247) to lay out the following factors applicable to springboard relief, based on a thorough review of the authorities, which have consistently been cited with approval in the more recent cases:

　　1)　Where a person has obtained a 'head start' as a result of unlawful acts, the court has the power to grant an injunction which restrains the wrongdoer, so as to deprive him of the fruits of his unlawful acts. This is often known as 'springboard' relief.

　　2)　Springboard relief is not confined to cases of breach of confidence. It can be granted in relation to breaches of contractual and fiduciary duties.

　　3)　Springboard relief must, however, be sought and obtained at a time when any unlawful advantage is still being enjoyed by the wrongdoer.

4) Springboard relief should have the aim simply of restoring the parties to the competitive position they each set out to occupy and would have occupied but for the defendant's misconduct.

5) Springboard relief will not be granted where a monetary award would have provided an adequate remedy to the claimant for the wrong done to it.

6) Springboard relief is not intended to punish the defendant for wrongdoing. It is merely to provide fair and just protection for unlawful harm on an interim basis.

7) The burden is on the claimant to spell out the precise nature and period of the competitive advantage. An 'ephemeral' and 'short term' advantage will not be sufficient.

10.7.6.   The court must consider how long the advantage will last and limit the duration of the injunction to that length of time. The Court said it is not intended to punish a defendant for wrongdoing.

10.7.7.   The advantage must still exist at the time the injunction is sought and it must be shown that it would continue unless restrained. It is to protect against future loss and must not be used to punish breaches of contract: *Clear Edge v Elliot* [2011] EWHC 3376 (QB) para 54.

10.7.8.   A good example of the length of the springboard restraint is in *Dorma v Bateman & Ors* [2016] IRLR 616 involving a team move where only one of the four defendants had restrictive covenants. The injunction restrained them all from working in the same business in the UK market and from soliciting specified customers. However, the length of the 'springboard' injunction for the other three defendants matched the six-month non-competition PTR in the first defendant's contract.

10.7.9. *MPT Group v Peel* [2017] IRLR 1092 provides a good example of the way a court assesses the length of a springboard advantage. In that case, as a result of this assessment, the claimant company was denied the relief they wanted. MPT produced mattresses. Two employees incorporated M Ltd, a direct competitor, as soon as their six months restrictive covenants ended in March 2017. They had copied significant amounts of their employer's information, including downloading databases of sales quotations, suppliers, materials and costs and technical drawings. These were clear breaches of the duty of fidelity. It was alleged that they were able to set up three mattress-making machines almost immediately after the incorporation of M Ltd due to this information. An application for an interim springboard injunction was made in June 2017, whereby MPT sought springboard injunctions until May 2018. The court decided that by the time of a trial in October 2017, any springboard advantage would have ended. They looked at the defendants' drive to succeed, their access to metal components and their capacity to focus on design and production. They decided any springboard advantage would have ended by September. Because there would be nothing to restrain by the time of trial, it was right for the Court to look at the merits at the stage of interim relief.

10.7.10. Having established the evidence showed they did not copy MPT's machine, the Court refused to grant a springboard injunction to stop their operation. The essential reason was that the case was based on inference and it was unlikely MPT could establish sufficient misuse of its information to justify a springboard injunction at trial. The Court did grant a lesser injunction limited to stopping them from using confidential information they had taken (effectively copying

MPT's machine), which they claimed not to have done in any event.

10.7.11. Another recent example of the court assessing the length of the springboard advantage can be found in *Aquinas Education v Miller* [2018] IRLR 518. This case also illustrates that the advantage may not in fact be very long. The claimant was a recruitment agency for teachers for whom two defendants worked. Whilst still employed they set up a company ("Newco") with a view to competing. Newco was also a defendant. They copied to a memory stick the claimant's records containing contact information on teachers and schools. The defendants approached teachers identified from the records and tried (and in some cases succeeded) to place them with schools on behalf of Newco. The defendants resigned on notice. On 12 January 2018, the day before their notice expired, the claimant obtained an interim springboard injunction that inter alia precluded them from doing business with teachers on the copied records. A further interim hearing on 26 February 2018 had to decide whether that would continue.

10.7.12. The Court noted that they had had a springboard advantage but that had come to an abrupt halt when the injunction had been granted on 12 January. They had planned to do a mail shot with the stolen details which would have gained them a very considerable advantage, but had not got that far. The situation had to be compared with what would have happened had there been no advantage. They had no PTRs and could therefore have set up the business on 14 January 2018. On the evidence, the temporal length of the head-start which the defendants obtained from their unlawful activity was in the region of six weeks. The orders already made had effectively restrained the defendants from what would otherwise have been lawful trading for a period of approximately six weeks, and any head start they had illegitimately obtained had gone. The springboard injunction was not continued.

10.7.13.   By contrast, in *Seatreiver International Holdings v Daly* [2018] EWHC 2424 (Ch), a 12-month springboard injunction was granted, but only in relation to a limited number of clients.

Court of Appeal's recent comments on springboard

10.7.14.   In *Forse v Secarma* [2019] EWCA Civ 215 the Court of Appeal commented on the powerful effect of a springboard injunction and also looked at the considerations relevant to its length. This is discussed in detail at paragraphs 6.2.3 to 6.2.7 above.

10.8.   <u>Garden leave injunctions</u>

10.8.1.   'Garden leave' is the term coined to describe the suspension of an employee in order to protect the employer's trade secrets and connections. Generally speaking, employers only resort to garden leave when a senior executive or other key employee has announced his wish to leave his or her employment and the employer is concerned that they may join a competitor. Less commonly, garden leave may be used where it is the employer that has decided to terminate the employment. In either event, the employee is usually required to serve notice of termination whilst not attending work (which can be a period of months or even a year or more) or, less usually, they may be required to stay at home during the remainder of their fixed-term employment contract.

10.8.2.   Should an employee who has been asked to take garden leave disregard this instruction and commence work with the competitor, the employer's primary remedy is an injunction to restrain the employee working for the competitor and holding him or her to the contract. If the employer wishes to obtain an injunction on the basis of the restrictions in its existing employment contract, the employer must avoid accepting the breach of contract which the employee has committed by leaving without giving notice. Instead the employer must affirm the employment contract by declaring that he does not accept the employee's breach as terminating the relationship and that the employer wishes to perform its obligations and wishes to hold the employee to the contract.

Payment during a garden leave injunction?

10.8.3.   In *Sunrise Brokers LLP v Rodgers* [2015] ICR 272 the Court of Appeal held that the fact the employer was not willing/offering to pay wages during the notice period did not prevent them obtaining an injunction to hold the employee, who wished to leave immediately, to his contract during the notice period. They found that the trial Judge's decision to this effect was a correct decision on the facts because the employee was not ready and willing to work. In *Sunrise*, the Court also distinguished a garden leave injunction (which is permissible) from an injunction forcing an employee to work for the employer (which could never be granted).

Considerations of the court in deciding whether to grant a garden leave injunction

10.8.4.   In *Finn v Thomas Brook Holliday* [2014] IRLR 102 (Simler J) the defendant employee indicated an intention to resign but the employer exercised its express contractual right to place him on garden leave on a 12-month notice period. The defendant resigned summarily, alleging there had been a repudiatory breach of contract by the employer and stating he intended to take up the employment. The employer sought and obtained an interim injunction restraining the defendant from taking up the employment, pending a speedy trial.

10.8.5.   At trial, having found there was no repudiatory breach by the claimant employer, the Court considered whether it was appropriate to grant an injunction to enforce or aid the period of garden leave. That had to be considered in light of the restraint of trade doctrine; the claimant still had to show there was a legitimate interest to protect and that the injunction extended no further than was necessary to protect it. Here the interest was customer connection as the defendant had built up strong connections during his 14 years working for the claimant. The claimant needed a reasonable time to build up its own relationships and on the evidence, 12 months was the minimum period necessary

10.8.6. The decision in *Elsevier v Munro* [2014] IRLR 766 was to the same effect and the facts were very similar to those in *Finn*. It was found that the defendant had waived any breach of contract he relied on, so the contract remained in being and contained a provision that he should not be engaged in any business in competition during his employment. Importantly, Warby J held that an injunction would be granted without proof that the employee would misuse his confidential information. Here the defendant retained confidential information in his memory. Whilst he would not deliberately misuse it, there was a real risk he would do so unconsciously and he would foster the competitor's business in areas where it was in competition with the claimant.

10.8.7. In *ICAP Management Services v Dean Berry* [2017] IRLR 811, the High Court held that the correct approach to the question of enforcement of garden leave was that set out by Simler J in *Finn*.

10.8.8. In practice, much of the argument in cases concerning injunctions to enforce garden leave provisions relates to whether the employer is itself in repudiatory breach of contract, which would mean that it cannot then rely on the garden leave provisions. In *Andrew Faieta v Management Services* [2017] EWHC 2995 (QB), a case in which there was an express garden leave clause, the High Court held that there was an implied term that the employer would not exercise its discretion to place the employee on garden leave irrationally or perversely. However, that had not been breached on the particular facts.

An alternative approach: affirmation and a declaration of continued employment during the notice period

10.8.9.   In the recent case of *Square Global Ltd v Leonard* [2020] EWHC 1008 (QB) the Court took a different approach to holding the employee to his notice period, but achieved broadly the same result as a garden leave injunction.

10.8.10.   The defendant, a broker for Square, resigned summarily on 11 November 2019. His employment contract required him to give six months' written notice of termination and included a non-competition covenant for a period of six months after the termination of his employment. The same day, his line manager emailed him to explain that he did not accept that he was entitled to resign without notice. He asked him to come back to work the following day. Square consistently took the position that the defendant remained an employee. The court rejected the defendant's argument that he had been constructively dismissed and hence released from his contract.

10.8.11.   The Judge accepted that this amounted to an affirmation of the contract by Square and that the contract entitled them to require Mr. Leonard not to work for a third party until the expiry of his six months' notice. He granted them the relief they sought, namely a declaration that the defendant remained an employee until 11 May 2020, coupled with an order prohibiting the defendant from undertaking competitive employment or any other form of work with a third party while he remained an employee of Square. In addition, the Judge granted a further injunction enforcing the six-month non-competition covenant, so the employee was prevented from competing with Square until 11 November 2020.

10.8.12.   This was in substance exactly the same type of relief as was granted in the *Sunrise Brokers LLP v Rodgers* case referred to above, where the Court of Appeal approved the mechanism of holding the employee to his contract after resignation in breach of contract, following an affirmation of the contract by the employer. However, the point to emphasise is that the decision in *Square Global* is not made with reference to any garden leave provisions in the contract. This would suggest that a declaration and injunction upholding the notice period alone is sufficient to stop the employee competing and hence, that injunctions in this area are not confined to the enforcement by the courts of express garden leave provisions.

Summary of the law on garden leave injunctions

10.8.13.   The bullet points below set out a summary of the legal issues arising in relation to garden leave injunctions, derived from the recent cases.

i   Where an employer has put an employee on garden leave and then seeks an injunction to prevent an unwilling employee from joining a competitor before the expiry of his notice period, an injunction to enforce and aid that period of garden leave must be considered in light of the restraint of trade doctrine.

ii   In some such cases, express restraints in the contract are being enforced by the garden leave injunction; in other cases the implied duty of fidelity is used as a basis for the injunction during the currency of the contract.

iii There are some earlier decisions to the effect that a restriction on working for a competitor during employment is not subject to the restraint of trade doctrine. Nevertheless, Underhill LJ in *Sunrise Brokers* said that the courts would be "very ready to enforce" the duty of fidelity.

iv   In *Finn*, Simler J said that restraint of trade did not normally apply to restrictions during the contract and garden leave, but the principles would be engaged "where an employer has put an employee on garden leave and then seeks an injunction to restrain an unwilling employee from joining a competitor". This was because of the scope for abuse by employers of a garden leave provision, which she said was "well recognised" (para 56-57). It is a weapon in the hands of an employer that might be used to ensure that an ambitious employee will not give notice if he is going to be unable to work at all for a long period of notice.

v   Simler J said that the fact the employee agreed to the garden leave provisions was only "a factor in the court's consideration", not the primary factor.

vi   Accordingly, an injunction sought to aid or enforce garden leave must be justified on similar grounds to a restrictive covenant.

vii   There is however greater flexibility to cut down the period of the restraint to less than the full notice period than there is when dealing with the duration of an injunction based on a restrictive covenant.

viii   Whereas the enforceability of a restrictive covenant is to be judged at the time it was entered into, the court looks at the issue of garden leave at the time enforcement is sought.

ix   In light of *Square Global Ltd v Leonard*, it appears to be immaterial whether there is an express garden leave clause where an employer is seeking to hold an employee to the restrictions of his/her employment contract within his/her contractual notice period.

x   Finally, it is important to emphasise that an employee also has a cause of action available to him or her. An employee who considers he or she is subject to the unreasonable imposition of garden leave by the employer, in breach of the restraint of trade doctrine, has the option of seeking a declaration as to the enforceability of the contract terms which the employer relies upon.

10.9.   The length of a garden leave injunction

10.9.1.   If the court is persuaded that there is a sufficiently serious risk, it will grant an injunction for the minimum period it considers necessary to protect the first employer's legitimate interest, which will not necessarily be for the remaining period of the employment contract.

10.9.2.   However, for a recent case where the court held an employee to the full 12 months of his garden leave period, see *ICAP Management Services v Dean Berry* [2017] EWHC 1321 (QB) (supra).

10.9.3.   Injunctions are sometimes sought to restrain an employee from working for a competitor for the duration of restrictive covenants after the end of the garden leave. In *Credit Suisse Asset Management Ltd v Armstrong* [1996] IRLR 450 it was stated that a court might decline to enforce a restrictive covenant where a long period of garden leave has already elapsed. However, in *Tradition Financial Services v Gamberoni & Ors* [2017] EWHC 768 (QB) a PTR preventing an inter-dealer broker in the energy market from working for competitors for six months was held to be reasonable, even if he were placed on garden leave for three months prior to termination, resulting in a nine month absence from brokering.

CHAPTER ELEVEN
DRAFTING, INTERPRETING AND ENFORCING EXPRESS RESTRICTIONS – SOLICITATION, COMPETITION AND CONFIDENTIAL INFORMATION

Solicitation, competition, confidential information and other clauses

11.1.   Background: the restraint of trade doctrine

11.1.1.   The restraint of trade doctrine is the principle that an individual should be free to follow his or her trade and use his or her skills without undue interference. The principle renders a contractual term purporting to restrict an individual's freedom to work for others or carry out his or her trade or business (a restrictive covenant) void unless it is designed to protect specific legitimate business interests and no wider than reasonably necessary to do so. The doctrine has a long history in English common law dating back many centuries.

11.1.2.   The law on interpretation and enforceability of restrictive covenants was given a recent steer in the decision in *Egon Zehnder Ltd v Tillman* [2020] AC 154 (SC), handed down in July 2019. This is the first time in a century that the UK Supreme Court, or the House of Lords, has considered restrictive covenants. The key areas of interest in *Tillman* relate to the issue of severance and the question of the proper approach to the construction of covenants. A further issue in the case was the proper scope of the doctrine of restraint of trade, although arguably the decision did little to advance understanding in this area. However, the importance of *Tillman* is such that this chapter includes a detailed analysis of it, prior to considering the current state of the law on severance and construction. It is acknowledged that there are many issues relating to restrictive covenants which fall outside the scope of *Tillman* and that it is therefore also necessary to consider other cases.

11.2.   <u>The most common forms of restrictions</u>

a   'Non-competition' clauses (containing a prohibition on competing, often limited to a certain geographical area)

b   'Non-solicitation' clauses (preventing the solicitation of the ex-employer's customers and/or suppliers)

c   'Non-dealing' clauses (like non-solicitation clauses, but, where there is a very personal customer relationship, recognising that it may be hard to prove who contacted who, this type of clause goes further and seeks to prevent all dealing between the ex-employee and customers and/or suppliers)

d   'Non-poaching' clauses (preventing the ex-employee from trying to poach other members of the employer's staff)

e   'Confidential information' clauses (preventing the ex-employee from using/disclosing certain classes of information deemed to be confidential; there is usually also a clause requiring delivery up of all company property, documents and electronically stored information upon termination).

11.3.   <u>The key to understanding</u>

11.3.1.   Whether you want to draft an effective covenant from scratch, or have been asked to advise on the strength of an existing covenant, two key points must be understood:

i)   the court's approach to covenants;

ii)   the detailed facts of your client's business.

11.4. The court's approach to restrictive covenants

11.4.1. The first stage is to construe the clause. The second stage is a consideration as to whether or not the clause protects a legitimate interest, and if it does protect a legitimate interest, the third stage is to consider whether it is reasonable and, moreover, no wider than is reasonably necessary.

11.5. First stage: Principles of construction

11.5.1. This is often not as simple as it sounds. Not only are some clauses poorly drafted and ambiguous; even well drafted clauses may give rise to matters of construction: what, for example, is the meaning of "a prospective customer"? Indeed, in order to come to a view as to what a clause means, the court may have to determine disputed facts. There are two important general statements of principle:

i   "...*in the construction of a covenant in restraint of trade, the same principles are to be applied as in the construction of any other written term...*" – Chadwick LJ, *Arbuthnot Fund Managers v Rawlings* [2003] AER (D) 181.

ii   "...*Interpretation is the ascertainment of the meaning which the document would convey to a reasonable person having all the background knowledge which would reasonably have been available to the parties at the time of the contract.... The meaning which a document (or another utterance) would convey to a reasonable man is not the same thing as the meaning of its words. The meaning of words is a matter of dictionaries and grammars; the meaning of the document is what the parties using those words against the relevant background would reasonably have been understood to mean*": *Investors Compensation Scheme Ltd. v. West*

Bromwich Building Society [1998] 1 WLR 896 at 912H-913E.

11.5.2. Broadly speaking, the cases on the correct approach to construction of covenants demonstrate a tension between a literalist approach, where the court will not step in to assist an employer if the clause is poorly drafted, and a commercial approach, where notwithstanding the precise language used, the court is prepared to give words a commercially sensible interpretation. Some important aspects of the principles of construction were considered by the Supreme Court in 2019 in *Egon Zehnder Ltd v Tillman*. The proper approach will be analysed in detail below in the light of the *Tillman* decision.

11.6.   Second stage: Legitimate interest

11.6.1. The employer's claim for protection must be based upon the identification of some advantage or asset inherent in the business which can properly be regarded as, in a general sense, his property, and which it would be unjust to allow the employee to appropriate for his own purposes, even though he, the employee, may have contributed to its creation. (per Lord Wilberforce in *Stenhouse Ltd. v. Phillips* [1974] AC 391).

11.7.   Third stage: Width of clause

11.7.1. The covenant must be reasonable and no wider than is reasonably necessary:

> "*[I]t must afford no more than adequate protection to the benefit of the party in whose favour it is imposed*".

(per Lord Parker in *Herbert Morris v. Saxelby* [1916] AC 688)

11.7.2. Although in the more recent cases the reference is to "reasonable necessity", "*[r]easonable necessity is to be assessed from*

the perspective of reasonable persons in the position of the parties
as at the date of the contract having regard to the contractual
provisions as a whole and to the factual matrix to which the con-
tract would then realistically be expected to apply" (per Cox J in
TFS Derivatives v. Morgan [2005] IRLR 246).

11.8.   Some very important context

11.8.1.   First, unless the clauses are so badly drafted that the claim is
hopeless, there is generally little scope for a defendant arguing
about their enforceability on an application for an interim
injunction. Nevertheless, the court should deal with issues of
construction at the interlocutory stage (*Arbuthnot Fund Man-*
agers v Rawlings [2003] EWCA Civ 518 para 9 & 20). It is
often safer for an employee on the receiving end of an
injunction application to assume that the clauses will be
enforced. The question at this stage will be whether it is plain
and obvious that the clauses cannot be enforced having
regard to the well-known restrictions on restraint of trade. If
it is not plain and obvious, the clauses will be regarded as
having a reasonable prospect of being upheld and the courts
will grant appropriate injunctions. A recent example of this
principle is found in *Foration Ltd v Acfield* [2018] EWHC
2660 (QB), where the only challenges made by the
defendants to an interim injunction were the enforceability of
covenants and whether they had been breached. The court
said these were matters for trial and awarded an interim
injunction enforcing the covenants.

11.8.2.   Second, commercial contracts, such as contracts for the sale
and purchase of a business, often include restrictive covenants
applying to the parties to the deal to prevent them taking
away goodwill, confidential information and/or clients once
the deal is concluded. It has been stated in numerous cases[1]

---

1 for example *Kores v Kolock* [1959] Ch 109; *Cavendish v Makdessi* [2013] 1 All ER
(Comm) 787 at para 15 and 23.

that covenants signed in a commercial contract outside the employment sphere are more likely to be enforced. This point is considered in more detail below under "Competition clauses in goodwill agreements".

11.8.3.   Third, the Court of Appeal has deprecated the use of clauses in a standard form clearly intended to apply in the widest range of situations rather than being formulated in a way which focuses on the particular restraint necessary in respect of a particular employee. The use of standard clauses by employers, whilst common, is extremely risky. The correct approach to drafting clauses is on a bespoke basis, which takes into account the position of the employee and creates restrictions which are no wider than necessary to protect the employer's identified legitimate interest.

11.9.   <u>*Egon Zehnder Ltd v Tillman* in the Supreme Court in 2019</u>

11.10.   <u>Background</u>

11.10.1.   In 2004, Ms Tillman was employed as a consultant by Egon Zehnder ("EZ UK"), which is the UK arm of a global executive recruitment company. In 2012, she became the joint global head of its Financial Services Practice Group. Clause 13.2.3 of her employment contract contained a six-month non-competition covenant ("the NCC") that she would not

> "Directly or indirectly engage or be concerned or interested in any business carried on in competition with any of the businesses of the Company or any Group Company which were carried on at the Termination Date or during the period of 12 months prior to that date with which you were materially concerned during such period."

11.10.2.   In 2017, Ms Tillman's employment with EZ UK ended. She sought employment with a US firm, whilst contending that the NCC was an unreasonable restraint of trade and thereby void. EZ UK sought an interim injunction to enforce the NCC.

11.10.3. The difficulty for EZ UK was that her employment contract expressly permitted her to have up to a 5% shareholding in any company. The company could not reasonably argue that it had a legitimate interest in having a wider restriction after the end of employment than during it, so if this is what the clause meant and it could not be severed, it was in unlawful restraint of trade.

11.11. Procedural history

11.11.1. In the High Court, Ms Tillman argued that the requirement that she not be 'interested' in any of the competing businesses specified in the NCC prohibited her from having even a small minority shareholding in such a business. EZ UK contested this argument on the basis that:

1   correctly construed, the NCC did not prohibit her from having a minority shareholding in such businesses;

2   if the NCC did prohibit such a shareholding, the words 'or interested' should be severed and removed, leaving the rest of the clause intact.

11.11.2. Mann J agreed with EZ UK that the words 'or interested' did not have the effect of prohibiting Miss Tillman from holding shares in the relevant competing businesses. Consequently, the NCC was held not to be an unreasonable restraint of trade. He therefore did not make a decision on severance. Ms Tillman appealed.

11.11.3. The Court of Appeal found that the words 'or interested' did extend to prohibit shareholding and as a result the NCC was an unreasonable restraint of trade. Having reached this conclusion, it refused to sever the words 'or interested.' Consequently, Ms Tillman's appeal was upheld.

11.12.   Supreme Court judgment

11.12.1. The Supreme Court considered three issues:

1) if the NCC did prohibit shareholding, was that aspect of the NCC covered by the restraint of trade doctrine ("the Doctrine") at all?

2) correctly construed, did the words 'interested in' prohibit any shareholding?

3) if they did prohibit shareholding, could they be severed so as to leave the rest of the NCC intact?

11.13.   Issue 1: Scope of the doctrine

11.13.1. This issue could have been fundamental as EZ UK were effectively challenging the whole scope of the Doctrine. The Supreme Court largely avoided clarifying its scope which means this issue could arise again in the future, although it has to be said that EZ UK's argument – that the NCC fell within the doctrine apart from the words "or interested in" which fell outside it – was novel.

11.13.2. EZ UK raised this issue for the first time before the Supreme Court. It argued that not every post-employment restriction will restrain trade and that here a prohibition against holding shares would not be covered by the Doctrine. The Supreme Court rejected this argument, applying the 'broad, practical, rule of reason approach' which had been adopted in *Proactive Sports Management Ltd v Rooney* [2011] EWCA Civ 1444 to determine whether the restraint of trade doctrine applied or not. They said as follows:

1   The terms of the NCC contained an acknowledgment that the restraints fell within the Doctrine. Two clauses in particular indicated that EZ UK considered the NCC in its entirety to be in restraint of trade: (1) under clause 13.3 Ms Tillman agreed that all the provisions of the NCC were 'fair and reasonable' (2) clause 13.4 provided that were any restriction held to be invalid, it should be severed.

2   It was not surprising that EZ UK should prohibit Ms Tillman from holding shares in a competing business to protect itself against competing activity. Even a minority shareholding might enable Miss Tillman to influence its operations.

3   The employment of top executives is often subject to conditions that the employee hold shares in their new employer.

11.13.3.   Arguably, part of Lord Wilson's reasoning on this matter is flawed. He justifies his conclusion that a prohibition on shareholding is in restraint of trade in part by reference to whether the contractual intention was that all the clauses were restraints, which is, at least in part, a subjective question. However, the question of whether a particular prohibition is in restraint of trade is surely an objective one that cannot be determined by reference to the intentions of the parties. For example, if the parties in this case had expressly agreed that the Doctrine did not apply in respect of the restraint against Ms Tillman's ordinary engagement by a competing business, undoubtedly the Doctrine would nevertheless apply.

11.13.4.   However, Lord Wilson did then go on to provide some substantive reasons why a prohibition against shareholding might constitute a restraint of trade (at para 33, summarised at (2) and (3) above).

11.14. <u>Issue 2: Proper construction of the non-competition clause</u>

11.14.1. EZ UK contended that the words "interested in" did not encompass having a shareholding. This was their answer to the fact that the prohibition on having any shareholding would be in unlawful restraint of trade.

11.14.2. In determining the proper construction of the NCC, the Supreme Court first considered the extent of the 'validity principle'. According to this principle, where a clause in a contract is capable of having two meanings, one of which would result in its being void and the other its being valid, the latter is to be preferred. Some cases suggest the principle only applies when the two meanings are equally plausible; others take a broader approach. Lord Wilson adopted the approach in *Tindall Cobham 1 Ltd v Adda Hotels* [2014] EWCA Civ 1215 which said that for the two meanings/validity principle to apply, there must be another interpretation which is 'realistic'. It did not follow that they must have equal plausibility.

11.14.3. In the instant case, the Supreme Court rejected EZ UK's contention that the words 'or interested' did not cover shareholdings for two main reasons:

1   the obvious natural meaning of the word 'interested' covers shareholdings and this fact has been acknowledged in the case law since the nineteenth century;

2   EZ UK provided no alternative construction of the word 'interested' at all, let alone a 'realistic' one.

11.15. <u>Issue 3: Severance</u>

11.15.1. In respect of severance, the Supreme Court considered the two distinct approaches taken in *Attwood v Lamont* [1920] 3 KB 571 and *Sadler v Imperial Life Assurance Company of*

Canada [1988] IRLR 388, as applied in *Beckett Investment Management Group Ltd v Hall* [2007] ICR 1539 (CA). Under *Attwood,* severance of a covenant would only be available where it was "not really a single covenant but [was] in effect a combination of several distinct covenants", hence parts of a single covenant could not be severed. Under *Beckett,* a three-stage tests is adopted: as Lord Wilson sets out, under this test severance is available where

1   "The unenforceable provision is capable of being removed without the necessity of adding to or modifying the wording of what remains" (the 'blue pencil' test);

2   "The remaining terms continue to be supported by adequate consideration"; and

3   "The removal of the unenforceable provision does not so change the character of the contract that it becomes "not the sort of contract that the parties entered into at all.""

11.15.2.   The Court of Appeal had reconciled the two approaches by holding that the requirement for separate covenants established in *Attwood* was reflected in the third stage of the *Beckett* test. The Supreme Court rejected this approach and criticised the *Attwood* test as unsatisfactory for, amongst other things, the subjectivity of the question whether there was one covenant or several, and overruled it. Whilst noting that the 'blue pencil' test could operate capriciously, they adopted the *Beckett* approach but modified the third limb so that the final criterion of the test became

"whether removal of the provision would not generate any major change in the overall effect of all the post-employment restraints in the contract".

11.15.3.   Lord Wilson added that at this stage, the focus should be on the "legal effect of the restraints," and not on their "perhaps changing significance for the parties and in particular for the employee." The removal of the words did not generate a major change in the meaning of the contract. Applying the modified *Beckett* test, the Supreme Court found that the words "or interested" could be severed so that the rest of the NCC could be enforced.

11.16.   <u>The correct approach to severance following *Tillman* in the Supreme Court</u>

Clarity on which test

11.16.1.   The correct test to be applied when deciding questions of severance is the three-stage approach identified in *Beckett* (subject to the 'major change' modification). The Supreme Court overruled the decision in *Attwood*. Its requirements were held to be "instantly controversial and ultimately unsatisfactory". Consequently, *Tillman* has brought certainty as to the status of *Attwood* following *Beckett*.

11.16.2.   However, the *Attwood* test had already largely fallen out of use for some time before the Supreme Court's decision in *Tillman*. It seems to have been dispensed with in *Beckett* itself and in *Advantage Business Systems Ltd v James Hopley* [2007] EWHC 1783 (QB), HHJ Richard Seymour QC had gone so far as to state: "The guidance of Younger LJ in *Attwood v Lamont* [1920] 3 KB 571 at page 593… is apparently no longer to be followed." Renewed uncertainty around the application of the *Attwood* test appears largely to have developed only following the Court of Appeal's decision in *Tillman*.

Public Policy concerns

11.16.3.   A narrow approach to severance leads to the risk of the employee opportunistically benefitting from a few ill-chosen words, depriving the employer of important protection, despite having striven to frame an appropriate restriction. A generous approach to severance would allow employers to keep an excessive clause hanging over the employee's head indefinitely, knowing it could be severed.

11.16.4. In *Marshall v NM Financial Management Ltd* [1997] IRLR 449, Jonathan Sumption QC (as he then was, sitting as a Recorder) suggested that a fourth stage be added to the *Beckett* test: that severance "must be consistent with the public policy underlying the avoidance of the offending part". This condition was treated as a requirement in *TFS Derivatives Ltd v Morgan* [2005] IRLR 246 and in *UK Power Reserve Limited v Read* [2014] EWHC 66 (Ch). Lord Wilson acknowledged the existence of the fourth stage described in *Marshall* but chose not to include this extra step in his reformulation of the *Beckett* test.

11.16.5. The inclusion of a public policy brake might have been one way of creating a more balanced test that would prevent employers who had behaved oppressively or had deliberately drafted post-termination restraints in the widest way possible from successfully obtaining severance.

11.16.6. Lord Wilson did go some way to acknowledging this issue. He cited (at para 78) *Freshasia Foods Ltd v Lu* [2019] EWHC 638 (Ch) in which Arnold J said that the law should not allow an employer first to extract an unreasonably wide covenant from an employee inhibiting him from leaving work to go elsewhere and then, if challenged, to secure easily its removal and the enforcement of the remainder. He also said (at para 66) that the law should take a cautious approach to severance of a PTR, for good public policy reasons. It is however questionable how far these concerns are reflected in his decision on the law.

Ongoing difficulties with the 'Major Change' stage

11.16.7.   Lord Wilson considered that the third stage of the *Beckett* test was best formulated in terms of whether there would be any 'major change' in the overall effect of post-employment restraints following severance. However, no substantial guidance is given as to what might constitute a 'major change.' Moreover, it is unclear to what extent Lord Wilson's modification requires a different approach to that adopted in *Beckett* at the third stage.

11.16.8.   Presumably, the fact that covenants are contained in separate promises might be an indicator that the deletion of one of them would not bring about a 'major change' in the effect of the restraints but the Supreme Court did not comment on this point.

11.16.9.   As a matter of language, it would presumably be more difficult for an employer to convince a court that there has been no 'major change' in the effect of post-employment restraints than it would for it to assert that the contract is the same 'sort of contract that the parties entered into' in the first place.

11.16.10. Yet in *Tillman* itself, although the effect of severing the words 'or interested' on Ms Tillman's PTRs appears substantial, the Supreme Court permitted the clause to be severed. Without severance, the NCC would have prevented Ms Tillman holding any shareholding whatsoever in a relevant competing business. By contrast, with the severed words removed, she could hold up to 100% of the shares in a competitor. Lord Wilson observed that it was completely unsurprising that EZ UK would want to prevent Ms Tillman from holding shares in the relevant competitive businesses. He therefore seems to have acknowledged that a prohibition on shareholding might have been of real importance to EZ UK. Yet the jettisoning of the entire prohibition by severance, made necessary by the application of the 'blue pencil' test, was still not regarded as a 'major change'.

11.16.11. Further, the requirement that Ms Tillman not be 'interested in' competitive businesses was one of only three restrictions placed upon her by clause 13 (the others being the restraints against becoming engaged or concerned in a competing business). At paragraph 90, Lord Wilson goes on to state that it would have also been appropriate to remove the words 'or be concerned' if holding a passive shareholding in a company meant that one was concerned in it. Were he to have done so, the only restriction left in the NCC would have been the prohibition against becoming engaged in a competing business. Yet there would still have been no 'major change' in the effect of the covenants, despite the removal of two thirds of the restrictions in the NCC.

11.16.12. Consequently, it is suggested that whatever effect the modification to the third stage was intended to have, it is now if anything easier for employers to obtain severance of unreasonable restraints in restrictive covenants.

The practical effects

11.16.13. The ability of ex-employees to challenge non-competition and non-solicitation clauses on the basis they are too wide appears to be somewhat more limited than before. This is particularly the case where the clauses will still make sense if the offending words are simply removed.

11.16.14. Practical examples of this approach can be found in some of the cases which pre-date *Tillman*. In *Beckett*, two independent financial advisers had resigned from their employment with Beckett and established a competing business. The Court of Appeal upheld a non-dealing covenant by severing an extended definition of 'relevant client'.

11.16.15. A further example can be found in *TFS Derivatives v Morgan* [2005] IRLR 246, where the clause said the employee would not for "six months undertake, carry on or be employed, engaged or interested in any capacity in either any business which is competitive with or similar to a Relevant Business within the Territory, or any business an objective or anticipated objective of which is to compete with a Relevant Business within the Territory". The Judge considered that the words "or similar to" were too wide to protect a legitimate interest, but severed them and found the clause to be enforceable on that basis.

11.16.16. However, one practical restraint on the employer's ability to run a severance argument is that if the offending definition or provision applies to more than one covenant, it could be argued that its deletion will indeed lead to a major change in the effect of the covenants.

Costs

11.16.17. Although the test for severance appears to have been relaxed, it is noteworthy that there might be costs implications for employers in severance cases. Lord Wilson noted that there might be a 'sting in the tail' for employers in respect of costs. He cited approvingly the decision in *Freshasia Foods Ltd v Lu* [2018] EWHC 3644 (Ch), in which the Deputy Judge described the unreasonable parts of post-employment restrictions as 'legal litter' which may 'cast an unfair burden on others to clear them up.'

Express severance clauses

11.16.18. Many contracts contain a clause saying that if any part of the covenants are unenforceable, they can be severed leaving the remaining covenants intact. These do not add anything to the contract. The clause simply reflects the common law powers of the court to sever and does not add to the result: *UK Power Reserve v Read* [2014] EWHC 66 (Ch) at para 95.

11.16.19. Many older contracts contain a different type of clause which confers on the court a power to rewrite the contract by substituting such words (including different periods of time or area limitations) as the court thinks appropriate. This type of clause is ineffective: *Living Design Home Improvement v Davidson* [1994] IRLR 69 (CSOH). English courts have no power to rewrite a contract.

11.17.   The current approach to construction following *Tillman* in the Supreme Court

11.17.1.   When considering the issue of severance, Lord Wilson noted that each word in a covenant should be given effect and should be treated as having a content of its own.

11.17.2.   It should be emphasised that where there is difficult or ambiguous language, there are two possible scenarios:

(i)   where one of two possible interpretations of a clause will lead to the clause being unenforceable as in unlawful restraint of trade. This is where the 'validity principle' applies and was the situation in *Tillman*;

(ii)   where language is ambiguous and one possible interpretation will mean that the clause simply does not apply to the actions of the departing employee. This was not directly addressed in *Tillman*.

The validity principle.

11.17.3.   The Supreme Court in *Tillman* provided clarification on the extent of the validity principle. In future, the principle will apply when a party can provide a 'realistic' alternative interpretation of a provision. The interpretation least likely to render the clause void will then apply. Lord Wilson said in terms that to apply it whenever an element of ambiguity exists is to countenance too great a departure from the otherwise probable meaning. Indeed, Lord Wilson cited with approval Megarry J in *Inland Revenue Comrs v Williams* [1969] 1 WLR 1197 who said that just because an element of ambiguity existed, that did not countenance a departure from an otherwise probable meaning, if one construction was clearly preferable to the other. It must also follow that the validity principle will only have a role where there is *some* ambiguity in the meaning of a clause or word. If it is unambiguous, the only other avenue available to the court would be severance.

Constructions favouring one party or the other

11.17.4. The validity principle does not apply at all where there are rival constructions, but the covenant is not rendered more likely to be void or enforceable depending upon which applies. Nevertheless, one construction might favour the employer and another the employee. One construction could also be more plausible than another. Until recently, the courts tended to take an approach which gives precedence to the principle of freedom of contract over freedom of competition. In other words, regardless of the language used, they would give the clause a commercially sensible construction, which made it more likely to apply to the actions of the employee.

11.17.5. However, in *Prophet Plc v Christopher Huggett* [2014] IRLR 797 (CA), Rimer LJ re-emphasised that if the courts were going to intervene, there needed to be ambiguity in the language.

> "*If faced with a contractual provision that can be seen to be ambiguous in meaning, with one interpretation leading to an apparent absurdity and the other to a commercially sensible solution, the court will favour the latter. [This approach] can only be adopted in cases in which the language of the provision is truly ambiguous and admits of clear alternatives as to the sense the parties intended to achieve.*"

11.17.6. Where there is no ambiguity, if the effect of the covenant is that it does not cover the activity which the departing employee is engaged in, even if it is badly written, the court will not rewrite it so that it has effect. This was the situation in *Prophet Plc v Christopher Huggett*. The company developed and sold computer software designed for the fresh produce industry, and Mr Huggett was their sales manager. His contract contained a provision that he would not engage in a business that was similar to or competed with the company for 12 months after the termination of his employment, with a proviso that this would operate only in connection with products with which he was involved when employed. Mr Huggett had only been involved with two products whilst working there and they were products only sold by the company. The company was granted an injunction when Mr Huggett went to work with a competitor but this was overturned on appeal. The Court of Appeal held that the Judge at first instance had taken the incorrect approach in construing the clause, which said that Mr Huggett could not work with the specified products, by adding the words "or similar thereto". The restrictive covenant was an unambiguously clear, carefully drafted legal clause even if interpreting it literally meant it could have no practical effect.

11.17.7.   It is however relevant to note that recent decisions of the Supreme Court, in cases not involving employee competition, have not been consistent as to the degree to which commercial common sense (which in this context means what the parties were trying to achieve by mutually agreeing restrictions) can be invoked as a basis for departing from the literal meaning of words. In *Arnold v Britton* [2015] AC 1619, Lord Neuberger said that the reliance placed on commercial common sense and surrounding circumstances should not be used to undervalue the words of the provision being construed and the court cannot embark on an exercise of "searching for, let alone constructing drafting infelicities to facilitate a departure from the natural meaning".

11.17.8.   However, the subsequent Supreme Court case of *Wood v Capita Insurance Services Ltd* [2017] 2 WLR 1095 arguably suggests that there is greater scope for testing the language against its business sense. Lord Hodge, with whom the other Justices of the Supreme Court all agreed, said that ascertaining the objective meaning of the language is not a literalist exercise. The court is not just looking at the language used but also at the context in which it is drafted and where there are rival constructions to a clause, the court can take into account which construction is more consistent with "business common sense". However, *Wood* also suggests that the fact an agreement was evidently carefully drafted may leave less scope to depart from what appears to be the meaning which the words convey. Although neither *Wood* nor *Arnold* relates to the interpretation of restrictive covenants, these principles will be of general application to the construction of contracts.

11.18. Non-solicitation and non-dealing clauses

(i) what does solicitation mean?

11.18.1. An overarching definition was set out in *QBE v Dymoke & Ors* [2012] IRLR 458, where Haddon-Cave J referred to the "time-honoured test" that there needs to be a "specific and direct appeal".

11.18.2. The definition was considered in more detail in *Croesus Financial Services Ltd v Bradshaw* [2013] EWHC 3685 (QB). This was the 'speedy trial' of a claim in which the defendants were father and son employees of the claimant financial services company. The father, who was the first defendant, had brought in his son, the second defendant, with a view to the son taking over his client base. The second defendant resigned to work for a competitor and, according to the claimant, persuaded many of its clients to transfer to his new employer. Both the first and second defendants were subject to non-solicitation covenants under which they were forbidden for 12 months to compete or to "canvass or solicit or do business with any restricted person [a client or supplier of the company during the last two years] with whom you have had personal contact in the course of your duties".

11.18.3. The claim was for damages for breach of contract, inducing breach of contract and unlawful means conspiracy. The Court had to construe the non-solicitation clause.

11.18.4. The Court held that "personal contact in the course of [their] duties" meant contact more than trivial or *de minimis*, undertaken by the covenantor. It was not necessarily true that there was no solicitation where the former employee was contacted by the customer. Who made the contact was relevant though each case depended on its own facts. In this case, the second defendant's communications, even where the clients contacted him first, involved him persuading them to transfer their business. There was also evidence that the first defendant (who had not resigned) solicited business on behalf of the second defendant.

11.18.5. The outcome was that the unlawful means conspiracy was found proved. The first and second defendants had acted in concert in relation to the claimant's clients, motivated by unhappiness that the claimant had refused to allow the first defendant's commissions to be transferred to the second defendant. The claimant was awarded both £300,000 in damages and a limited injunction for the remainder of the 12-month period (to allow it to consolidate its position).

11.18.6. *Towry EL Limited v Bennett* [2012] EWHC 224 (QB) was a case that fell on the other side of the line from *Croesus*. The employer's claim failed because, against the background that the former employees had not made the first contact with the clients, the Court was not prepared to draw the inference that clients had moved to the competitor as a result of breaching the non-solicitation covenants. The Judge said that a key feature of solicitation was that "[a]n element of persuasion is required". The clause said that they would not:

> *"solicit, canvas or endeavour to solicit or canvas in any capacity whatsoever, by post, phone, electronic communication, personal contact, or by any other means, any business, orders or custom which is in competition with any restricted Business."*

11.18.7.   The fact that the defendants, who were financial advisers, believed clients wanted to follow them when they left their former employer did not mean there had been an intention to solicit those clients. The defendants were well aware of the covenants and had taken legal advice on how to avoid breaching them. Indeed, the fact that there had been meetings in which the ex-employees had advised clients on the benefits of their business model/ fee structure and encouraged or recommended transfer did not mean there had been solicitation, because in the circumstances of the case, the clients either did not regard the information conveyed to them as relevant or by the time the defendants were providing the advice, the Judge felt that the clients had already decided to retain their personal financial adviser and take their business away from the claimant.

11.18.8.   In *Ranson v Customer Systems Plc* [2012] IRLR 769, an ex-employee took a client out to dinner in his spare time before leaving his employment. There was no discussion of the client transferring his business. It was held that there had been no solicitation.

11.18.9.   The facts of *Argus Media v Halim* [2019] EWHC 215 (QB) are as set out above at paragraph 8.3.6. With regard to the non-solicitation restraints, the Judge considered whether the defendant had solicited certain clients. The Judge first noted that solicitation requires a "direct and specific appeal" and noted that in *Baldwin v Maidstone* (QBD) (Mercantile

Court) 3 June 2011, it was held that an advertisement in a local newspaper was not sufficiently targeted to amount to solicitation. The Judge first considered whether certain emails sent by the defendant's wife to a number of restricted clients before he resigned from his position amounted to solicitation on his part. He found that they were not, accepting that his wife had not sent the emails under the defendant's instruction. Nevertheless the defendant had deliberately 'turned a blind eye' to her actions, which amounted to a breach of his duty of fidelity.

11.18.10.   The Judge then turned to consider whether the defendant had solicited representatives of the International Fertilizer Development Centre— a restricted client— at a conference in Rwanda. The defendant argued that his discussions with the IFDC were purely social. In rejecting this contention, the Judge noted that the defendant had gone to Rwanda to build up his business and that there was a high degree of overlap between social and business interactions: "sometimes business relationships take many drinking sessions and meals over a long period of time to bear fruit." Further, there was in fact evidence that business matters were explicitly discussed. For these reasons, the defendant was found to have solicited the IFDC. The defendant was also found to have solicited a number of other restricted clients.

Definition of solicitation: Summary

11.18.11.   In summary, the requirement for an element of persuasion and a "direct appeal" to clients to transfer their business means that merely meeting or having phone contact will not of itself amount to solicitation. However, there is likely to be intense scrutiny of what was actually said or done in those communications. For an employee merely to state, in response to a question, that they will be trading from a particular place and doing the same kind of work is probably not enough to be soliciting. However, the suggestion that a client should or could transfer their business will probably cross the line. Conversely, the mere fact that the client has initiated the communication rather than the departing employee does not necessarily mean there has been no solicitation. It all depends on what was said.

11.18.12. These fine distinctions will not arise if the employer has included a non-dealing clause, instead of merely a non-solicitation clause. Depending on its precise wording, a non-dealing clause may have the effect that any dealings at all with the customer will breach the restriction and the employee would have to avoid having any kind of interaction.

(ii) Will a non-solicitation clause be effective if it covers customers with whom the claimant has not had contact?

11.18.13. When drafting a non-solicitation or non-dealing clause, it is sensible to limit its reach to clients with whom the relevant employee has had contact during the period prior to termination of the employment. This is frequently framed as a one or two-year period. Otherwise, there is a risk that the employee would argue that the clause is wider than necessary and therefore does not protect a legitimate interest, for various reasons. There is a danger of unwitting breach by the employee: depending on the work, they may be unaware that clients they deal with after termination were clients of the former employer. Also, depending on the industry, the employer may have no legitimate reason for keeping the employee away from those who may have been clients years before but are not current.

11.18.14. As a general rule, failing to limit the clause in this way creates a real danger that it could subsequently be struck down as being in unlawful restraint of trade, but there are exceptions. This point will be best illustrated by giving some examples.

11.18.15. In *Leonard Coppage & Freedom Security Solutions Ltd v Safetynet Security Ltd* [2013] IRLR 970 Company S was a security company employing security guards. The claimant was a director. His contract said he could not for six months following termination, directly or indirectly, in any capacity, approach any individual or organisation who had been a customer of S "during your period of employment... if the purpose of such an approach is to solicit business which could have been undertaken by us". The claimant resigned and within two weeks, five of S's customers had terminated their contracts and moved their business to company F, which had been incorporated on the same day as the claimant's resignation. S brought proceedings for breach of covenant and the Judge found the covenant reasonable and awarded damages. The claimant contended, among other things, that the covenant should have been restricted to the non-solicitation of customers from the last 12 months of his employment with S.

11.18.16. The Court of Appeal upheld the Judge's approach. The stability of S's customer list and the small minority of relevant customers from the last 12 months of the claimant's employment who had ceased to provide business to S showed that it was entirely reasonable to draft the covenant to relate to all customers within the entire period of the claimant's employment. The post-termination restraint period was only six months, which was a fundamental indication of reasonableness. As to the fact the covenant was not limited to clients with whom the claimant had dealt, the claimant was a key employee of S, the 'face' of the company, and in his latest role had been in contact with all of S's customers in the two years prior to his resignation. That indicated that he realistically had the power to influence those customers.

11.18.17. Another important factor was that account had to be taken of the limitation to the covenant provided by its concluding proviso: "if the purpose of such an approach was to solicit business which could have been undertaken by [S]". The use of "could" was not a reference to a mere theoretical possib-

ility, but to a commercially practical reality. The Court of
Appeal found it was reasonable to express the covenant in
that way, namely to assume that a customer from the period
of the claimant's employment was prima facie out of bounds,
for the strictly limited period of six months, subject to a
proviso that there was a commercially realistic possibility of S
providing services to the customers concerned (and if not,
solicitation of them would not have been a breach of covenant).

11.18.18. *Leonard Coppage* provides an interesting contrast with other
reported cases where the courts require non-solicitation covenants to be limited in scope to those clients with whom the
relevant employee had contact. Otherwise s/he might be
unwittingly in breach. An example is *WRN v Ayris* [2008]
IRLR 889 in which the relevant clause prevented the marketing manager in a telecoms company, for a period of 12
months, from seeking business, orders or custom from any
person to whom the company had supplied products during
the year prior to termination. It was not enforced.

11.18.19. The Court of Appeal in *Plowman v Ash* [1964] 1 WLR 568
said that there is no actual authority that there must have
been contact with customers to allow a proviso of this nature
to be upheld. Nevertheless, it is better to regard cases where
non-solicitation clauses not requiring contact have been
upheld as exceptions to the rule, based on their particular
facts.

11.18.20. In *Freshasia Foods Limited v Jing Lu* [2018] EWHC 2644
(Ch), the judge also considered the definition of "had
contact." The defendant was prohibited from soliciting
"restricted clients," who were defined as certain persons with
whom the defendant had "had contact" with during the 12
months ending on the date of termination of his
employment. The Judge concluded that "contact" meant
"material and not de minimis contact". He rejected the con-

tention that "contact" should refer to any contact because that was a non-commercial construction. On this basis, the clause in question was clearly not too wide. However, the Judge went on to say that even if "contact" was taken to refer to any contact, he would still have found the clause was not too wide "on the basis that it would remove arguments about the materiality of contact in the context of a clause limited to contact within the 12 months prior to termination."

(iii) Can potential customers fall within the scope of a non-solicitation clause?

11.18.21. There may be nothing wrong with a clause preventing an ex-employee from dealing with prospective customers with whom they have had discussions. However, even here, it depends on what is reasonable in a particular case and on the precise wording of the clause. Despite the fact that prospective customers are limited to those with whom the employee has had dealings, an employer may still struggle to show that they have a legitimate interest in excluding them where the negotiations with those customers failed.

11.18.22. In *Berry Birch and Noble Financial Planning v Berwick* [2005] EWHC 1803 (QB) the clause covered, inter alia, customers who had been in commercial negotiations with the employee with a view to placing business, even if those negotiations did not successfully result in business being placed. The Judge held that the business had no legitimate interest in relation to those who had never become its clients.

11.18.23. The decision in *Norbrook Laboratories v Adair* [2008] IRLR 878 was to the same effect. The defendant was the territory manager of a pharmaceutical company. A covenant provided, inter alia, that the claimant would not solicit or transact business with anyone who in the preceding period of two years had been a customer or prospective customer of the business *and* where the employee had access to or dealings with the prospective customer. There was no difficulty with this in relation to actual customers. However, the Court found on the facts that despite that limitation, the two-year backstop in respect of prospective customers was too broad, because those were persons whose custom Norbrook had failed to obtain and they may even be customers of a new putative employer. Ultimately this was not fatal to the employer's case because the judge 'blue pencilled' the words *"potential customer/s"*.

11.18.24. The position might be different, however, if the covenant was justified by the fact that the rapport which the employee built up with potential customers was part of the goodwill of the business or by the fact that it protected some special knowledge which the employee had over the customer base. For example, in *Gledhow Autoparts v Delaney* [1965] 1 WLR 1366 the Court of Appeal said that it was not fatal to a covenant that the employee, who was a salesman, had visited customers but they had not yet placed business with him. Helpfully, in *Associated Foreign Exchange v International Foreign Exchange (UK)* [2010] IRLR 964, Jeremy Cousins QC, sitting as a recorder in the Chancery Division, gave (at para 70) the following guidance as to when a covenant referring to prospective clients might be upheld:

> *"Of course there will be businesses in which protection in respect of potential customers is appropriate; for example where the building up of a relationship is a long and difficult process, perhaps involving protracted negotiation by a senior employee whose post-contractual solicitation of such potential customers it is sought to restrain. There may be circumstances in which attempting to establish relationships with potential customers has involved significant investment not only in time, but in money."*

11.18.25. It follows from this that if the covenant is not limited to those clients with whom there have been significant negotiations which have not yet born fruit, enforcement might be more difficult. The clause is also likely to face enforceability problems if the covenant extends beyond potential clients with whom the ex-employee had dealings to include those with whom, in the ex-employee's knowledge, other employees had dealings. A clause to this effect was regarded by the Court of Appeal in *Arbuthnot Fund Managers v Rawlings* [2003] EWCA 518 as being too broad.

(iv) Can clients which the employee initially brought to the employer be covered?

11.18.26.   Many if not most non-solicitation and non-dealing covenants make reference to clients without addressing the question of whether the employee brought those clients with him/her. Whilst it might seem unfair to prevent an employee from dealing with those clients after leaving, the employee may well have accepted a covenant in favour of his or her new employers which does not make this distinction and there is no doubt that during the employment they become the employer's clients.

11.18.27.   The case law on this issue can best be summarised by saying that the fact a covenant prevents an employee dealing with such customers for a limited period of time after the end of employment is a factor which the court is likely to take into account in deciding whether the employer has a legitimate interest to protect and whether the clause is no wider than necessary to protect it. However, in practice many of the cases are more nuanced than this. The following list provides a summary of the key points:

i.   Whether the restraint is reasonable will be determined partly by the question of what proportion of the clients as a whole are involved, as well as the extent and duration of the restriction.

ii. Where a more senior employee is involved, s/he is more likely to be taken to be fully aware of the restriction entered into: an example of where a covenant restricting a former managing director from dealing with several of 'his' customers was upheld by the Court of Appeal in these circumstances can be found in *Hanover v Shapiro* [1994] IRLR 82.

iii. In practice, the extent of the employer's legitimate interest in restricting dealings with such customers will be affected by the extent to which the employer has invested time and money in retaining them and providing services to them, as well as the period of time involved. In professions where the service all arises from one to one contact between client and employee, such as financial advisers, the employer may find it harder to argue that they have a legitimate interest.

iv. If the employee received a capital payment in relation to the customers, as in *Merlin Financial Consultants v Cooper* [2014] EWHC 1196 (QB), or if acquiring the customers was overtly part of the reason for the recruitment, again the employer's position will be easier to justify.

v. It is possible to avoid many of these difficulties by making specific reference to 'carried clients' and the employer's legitimate reasons for retaining them in a separate covenant.

11.19.   <u>"Non-competition" clauses</u>

a.i   When will a court decline to enforce a non-competition clause?

11.19.1.   Clauses saying that the departed employee may not be engaged in a business which competes with that of the former employer are draconian in effect because they may prevent the employee entirely from working in his/her chosen vocation. Traditionally, they have been difficult to enforce for this reason, particularly in cases where non-solicitation and non-dealing clauses provided adequate protection. An example of a non-competition clause being refused on that basis can be found in *Office Angels v Rainier Thomas* [1991] IRLR 214 (CA).

11.19.2. However, recently the courts have shown a greater tendency to uphold such clauses for middle-ranking and senior employees. There are two alternative rationales for doing so.

First rationale: protection of confidential information

11.19.3. The courts will enforce a covenant against competition if the employee has gained knowledge of the employer's processes or plans or knowledge of trade secrets which would potentially allow him/her to damage the previous employer or to give another business a competitive advantage by joining them and sharing that knowledge. For these purposes the relevant confidential information would include an advantage or asset inherent in the business (including information in the employee's head) which will enable a competitor to gain an edge. Even if the employee does not intend to use this knowledge, the courts have often found that there is a possibility s/he may do so unwittingly. Many employees have knowledge which they will use instinctively whilst doing their jobs, such as knowledge of the pricing structures or of the business strategies of other businesses.

11.19.4. An example is *Huw Thomas v Farr PLC* [2007] IRLR 419 where the employee had confidential information of the sort that the employer (a firm of specialised insurance brokers working in a relatively small market) had a legitimate interest in protecting, including business development plans and information about the potential for exploiting new areas of business and new geographical markets. The Court of Appeal gave very helpful guidance:

i   in order to establish that the inclusion of a non-competition clause in an employment contract was reasonably necessary for the protection of the employer's interest in confidential information, the first question is whether, at the time of entering into the contract, the nature of the proposed employment was such as would expose the employee to the kind of information capable of protection beyond the term of the contract.

ii   Provided that the employer overcomes that hurdle, it is no argument against a restrictive covenant that it may be very difficult for either the employer or the employee to know where exactly the line may lie between information which remains confidential after the end of the employment and information which does not. The difficulty in drawing the distinction may be the very reason why the non-competition clause is the most satisfactory form of restraint, provided that it is reasonable in time and space.

iii   In the instant case, the Court said that it might have been appropriate to refuse an injunction (as a matter of discretion – not because the clause was unenforceable) if the employee could not recall any truly confidential information, or if it was not of the nature that could be carried away in the employee's head, but that wasn't the case on these facts.

11.19.5.   From an employer's perspective, where confidential information is sought to be protected, a non-competition clause is a way of avoiding the need to get into very detailed arguments ex post facto as to what confidential information the ex-employee may or may not have had. Moreover, unlike the position with a confidentiality covenant, it is not necessary to identify in the covenant the information sought to be protected with precision; albeit the scope of the information would need to be identified in detail in due course if court proceedings are necessary.

11.19.6.   Other factors relevant to the enforcement of a clause in these circumstances include:

i   whether the terms of the covenant are appropriately limited, both as to the areas of business covered and limitations of time and space;

ii   the likely impact on the employee's ability to pursue their employment in their field of expertise;

iii the shelf-life of the confidential information, its importance and the period over which it was built up;

iv   the extent to which the information is likely to be memorable to the employee.

Second rationale: protecting customer connections and the difficulty of policing solicitation

11.19.7.   A more recent development in the courts is the tendency to uphold non-competition covenants where the justification for their use is the protection of customer connections. It is obviously possible to protect customer connections in most cases through non-solicitation and non-dealing covenants but in some circumstances those alone will not be adequate.

11.19.8.   The first situation is where a senior employee is not client-facing but could deal with former clients via members of his or her team. Here the issue is the difficulty of policing a non-solicitation or non-dealing covenant, as the solicitation will not be undertaken by the relevant employee but by subordinates. This was one of the bases upon which the covenant was upheld in *Hugh Thomas v Farr* (supra, at para 48 of the judgment). Mr Thomas, a managing director, did not as an individual deal directly with clients but those underneath him would be negotiating with them.

11.19.9. The second situation is where the fact that a senior employee or manager moves to another business is likely to cause clients to move to the same business, because of the reputation that individual has, even though those clients would be dealt with day to day by more junior staff. This situation is often referred to as 'natural gravitation'. In those circumstances, the senior employee would not have solicited them and he will not be dealing with them, but the employer still has a legitimate interest in protecting its existing client base.

11.19.10. This type of argument is, however, likely to be limited to very senior employees and in an ordinary case, it will be difficult to justify a non-competition covenant based on customer connection unless there is significant connection between the customer and defendant employee. In *QBE Management Services (UK) Ltd v Dymoke & Ors* [2012] IRLR 458, the claimant was a specialist marine insurer and the defendants were a group of senior employees who departed to set up in competition. However, some of the defendants were claims personnel and assistant or deputy underwriters and did not have regular client contact of the type enjoyed by the underwriters. The evidence did not support the contention that these employees had built up strong client relationships and therefore the Judge found that the evidence did not justify upholding non-competition covenants on that basis (see para 230 ibid).

11.19.11. Arguments about the difficulty in policing contact with former clients tend to involve trying to justify a covenant which is wider than that strictly necessary to protect a legitimate interest. In *Ashcourt Rowan Financial Planning v Hall* [2013] IRLR 637, where a six month non-competition covenant was struck down on that basis and also on the basis that the wording was wide enough to prevent the employee from being even indirectly concerned in the business activity of a competitor, the Court explained that in these circumstances a fact-sensitive assessment is required of the balance between the effect of restraints going beyond those tailored to protection and the need for additional restraint to police the covenant. The way this assessment was carried out in the *Ashcourt Rowan* case is considered below.

11.19.12.   Another interesting twist in relation to the issue of whether a non-competition clause can be justified by the need to protect client connections is provided by *Freshasia Foods Limited v Jing Lu* [2018] EWHC 2644 (Ch). In that case the Judge refused to uphold the 12 months non-competition clause on the basis that it was void for uncertainty, but went on to consider whether it would have been enforceable otherwise. In this case, as is not uncommon, the employer justified the 12-month duration by the fact that it was necessary because it required 12 months to build a customer relationship with a customer. The Judge rejected this justification because even if this were true, 12 months of protection would only be required if a customer had just become a customer at the end of the defendant's employment, in which case the defendant would have had little connection with them anyway. The evidence was that most of the customers had long-standing connections with the business.

Non-competition clauses in goodwill agreements

11.19.13.   It has been stated above that restrictive covenants in agreements relating to the transfer of goodwill, as opposed to employment contracts, are more likely to be enforced. This is because of an assumption that parties of equal bargaining power are best placed to determine the reasonableness of their covenants. It is also because of the principle that the seller should not derogate from the goodwill which has been sold. Despite this, depending on who the vendor and purchaser are, the restraint of trade doctrine is still likely to apply and the restriction still needs to be framed in a way which protects what has been acquired but is not unnecessarily restrictive.

11.19.14.   As the following case has demonstrated, it is important not to regard all share transfer agreements as the same, even if they are protecting goodwill. Some will have more in common with an employment contract than a commercial agreement.

11.19.15.   In *Ideal Standards International v Herbert* [2018] EWHC 3326 (Comm), the respondent was a senior employee for the Ideal Standards Group's main operating company. His employment contract contained confidentiality obligations. He was a party to a shareholders' agreement ("SHA") between five group companies. The SHA included a non-competition covenant. It also provided that any waiver of a term/ breach of the SHA would be in writing and signed by the granting party. The respondent was dismissed. He signed a settlement agreement with his employing company, which stated that the parties would have no obligations to each other, save what was provided for in the settlement agreement itself. The respondent began to work for a competitor. Two group companies applied for an injunction to enforce the non-competition covenant.

11.19.16.   The applicants submitted that non-competition clauses were more strictly enforced in shareholder agreements than in the ordinary employee context. However, the Judge found that this was not a simple matter of categorization in which employment agreement cases and shareholder agreement cases were treated differently. Rather, he considered that non-competition clauses in the context of a vendor of a partnership share or shares in a business will generally be enforced because these clauses are negotiated in a commercial context and have the legitimate aim of preventing the vendor attacking the goodwill of the partnership or business in question. By contrast, an ordinary employee might have a small shareholding in his employer's business, in which scenario these considerations do not apply. Consequently, the Judge held that the relevant test did not change because the defendant happened to have benefits which were shares.

Other reasonableness factors

11.19.17. The argument that a non-competition covenant should not be enforced if a non-dealing or non-solicitation covenant would be adequate is well established (see for example *CEF Holdings v Mundey* [2012] IRLR 912 at para 61). However, this was qualified in *QBE Management Services (UK) Ltd v Dymoke & Ors*, which said that it is only where the court finds that a "*much* less far-reaching" covenant would have afforded adequate protection that it is likely to regard the existing restriction as unreasonable (at para 216, quoting the Court of Appeal in *Office Angels v Rainer-Thomas*).

11.19.18. Although a duration of six or twelve months tends to be regarded as fairly standard where non-competition clauses are concerned, it certainly should not be thought that a court will accept that a six-month duration is reasonable, even in a case where an employer has a legitimate interest to protect. A recent example of this is *Monex Europe Limited v Pothecary* [2019] EWHC 1714 (QB), where it was also found that a world-wide restriction could not be justified. The question of the appropriate length of restraints is dealt with in detail below.

11.19.19. In *Monex*, the claimant company provided commercial Forex services for clients. The defendants worked for the claimant's sales team. They were subject to certain PTRs. A non-competition covenant prohibited them from working in any capacity in a business similar to the claimant's, in any market or exchange covered by the claimant, for six months following termination of their employment. The defendants left to work for a competitor. The claimant issued a claim for injunctive relief. The defendants offered undertakings that they would comply with their PTRs other than the non-competition covenant.

11.19.20.   Although the claimant had legitimate interests to protect – namely, confidential information and client connection – nevertheless the non-competition clause was void because it was in unreasonable restraint of trade. The Judge explained that the non-competition covenant required the defendants to be shut out entirely from working in the foreign exchange markets, anywhere in the world, for a period of six months. He stated that even if a non-competition covenant with a global reach was justifiable, there was no basis for contending that a six-month restraint was necessary. First, the shelf-life of the confidential information that the defendants could be expected to have access to was relatively short. Second, although the defendants could be expected to have an ongoing relationship with their clients, these were relationships that could be readily rebuilt by the claimant in a much shorter period than six months. Further, the global reach of the covenant was also unjustifiable: there was no evidence that the nature of the confidential information known to the defendants was truly global and no evidence that their client contacts were global. Finally, there was no evidence that the defendants' clients traded in many currencies. Consequently, only a much narrower covenant, in terms of geography, currency and the length of restraint, could have been justified.

11.19.21.   Where the employer seeks to protect confidential information by the non-competition covenant, for the purposes of going to court, the nature of that information will need to be identified as well as the reasons why its protection is sought. In the trial in *QBE Management Services* the claimants had gone to the trouble of particularising in a Scott schedule fourteen categories of confidential information which it said were confidential. However, the court found this was insufficient to justify the enforcement of the non-competition covenants on the grounds of access to 'trade secrets' or 'highly confidential' information. In particular, some were relatively basic, unsophisticated and not particularly secret; some contained unmemorable material of little practical advantage; much of it was publicly available in a similar form; and some was irrelevant to the role of the particular employee.

a.ii   Construing the contract: the meaning of "competition"

11.19.22.   This analysis of non-competition clauses relates to whether they are enforceable. However, as explained above the first step with restrictive covenants, prior to enforceability, is construction: what do they mean? Depending on the construction, it might be argued that the clause does not apply at all.

11.19.23.   One important issue is what is what is meant by "compete". This was relevant in *Phoenix Partner Group LLP v Asoyang* [2010] IRLR 594. The defendant had covenanted not to deal with clients or prospective clients of his former employer "in competition with the company" and not to be involved with a trade or business "which competes" for a period of six months following termination. His primary work for the claimant had been in the Euro Stoxx market, but after he left, the claimant stopped doing Euro Stoxx work. It had been actively recruiting for another Euro Stoxx broker to take the claimant's place, but it had not been successful. The Judge discharged an injunction as there was no prospect that within the three months which remained of the injunction the claimant would work in Euro Stoxx and hence there was no prospect at trial that the ex-employee would be found to have competed.

11.19.24.   To put this in context, in *Dawnay, Day & Co Ltd v D'Alphen* [1997] IRLR 442, the Court of Appeal held that a non-competition clause covered not only existing business but also other kinds of business which were in an advanced state of preparation by the former employer. Conversely, in *One Step*

Support Ltd v Morris-Garner [2015] IRLR 215[2], the High Court found that where the employer's plans to operate in a particular area were "dormant and unexpressed", that was not enough to place the employees, who had set up in that area, in breach of a non-competition covenant. Phillips J said

> *"One Step had not recruited, let alone trained staff. Nor had it established connections with potential commissioners, having neither applied for accreditation nor been invited to tender for business. There is no suggestion that One Step's managers were involved in considering any such matters. The most that can be said was that there had been a general intention to expand in that direction."*

11.19.25.   More recently, in *Gamatronic (UK) v Hamilton* [2017] BCC 670, the High Court[3] distilled the question of whether one entity was competing with another into the following considerations:

i   whether A (employer) and B (departing employee) are properly to be regarded as supplying goods and services which are sufficiently comparable to mean they are in competition;

ii   whether they compete in the same area;

iii   if they are not supplying the same products or services, was there a realistic prospect of them doing so?

iv   was the scope of A and B's business the same or was the scope of B's business within A's business plan?

---

2   The case was appealed to the Supreme Court, but not on these grounds.

3   Applying *One Step* in the Court of Appeal

11.19.26.   *Gamatronic* was then applied in *Argus Media Ltd v Halim* [2019] EWHC 42 (QB) The Judge cited the test applied in *Morris-Garner v One Step (Support) Ltd* [2017] QB 1 (which was overturned on appeal, but not in respect of this issue): "the essential question is whether the scope of the business was the same." He then noted that interchangeability was not a prerequisite to finding that two businesses were competitive. Rather, he needed to be satisfied that the products were either "similar" (*Morris-Garner* at para 59) or "sufficiently comparable" (*Gamatronic (UK) Ltd v Hamilton* [2016] EWHC at para 95).

11.19.27.   On this basis he found that the defendant's activities did amount to competition. In respect of the defendant's company Afriqom, its website indicated a desire to offer broader consultancy and training services, which were regarded to be within the scope of its business plan and so in competition with the claimant. He stated: "I take the view that the scope of the business of Afriqom is not limited to what it was doing at a snapshot of time. Thus, some of the material on its website was relevant to define the scope of its business which went beyond price assessments and beyond Africa [...]. In other words, the consultancy was more than merely some long-term hope, but was a part of the scope of the services which Afriqom intended to offer."

11.19.28.   The judgment in *Argus Media* indicates that the courts are willing to take a broad approach to the definition of competition. However, questions may arise in the future as to whether a particular project is a mere 'long-term hope' or part of the scope of the services provided by an allegedly competing company.

(iii)   In what capacity may the employee be involved in the competing business?

11.19.29. Another issue which is important both at the drafting stage and when construing the clause is the need for a clear definition of the capacity in which an employee can or cannot be involved in a competing business. Here the employer has to strike a balance between catching the employee's activities and not making the restriction so wide that it is unenforceable. Three examples illustrate the point:

11.19.30. In *Norbrook Laboratories v Adair* [2008] IRLR 878 the defendant was a salesperson for a pharmaceutical company. One of her PTRs said she could not be employed (etc.) in any "restricted business". Working in restricted business was defined as including involvement with products with which she was "concerned" in the last five years of her employment. That applied to a competing product with which she had no dealings other than as one of the many products she offered for sale, even if she had never sold it. That was held to be too wide to be enforceable. A separate issue was that the non-competition covenant was not limited to her taking up a role in a sales capacity but could have included any capacity in the business. However, the Court found the clause was not too wide on that basis. Confidential information could be revealed to a competitor irrespective of the capacity in which she was employed.

11.19.31. By way of contrast, in *Ashcourt Rowan Financial Planning v Hall* [2013] IRLR 637 the defendant was a senior financial adviser for a company providing financial advice. The fact that the non-competition covenant restricted involvement in a competitor business in a different capacity was found to make it too wide to be enforceable. The PTR stated that the defendant would not be "directly or indirectly engaged or concerned in any business or activity which competes directly with the business" with which he had been concerned during the previous 12 months. The court found that this covered being indirectly concerned in such activities by way of a management role, regulatory compliance, training, research into investment products and business development. It could not reasonably be said that the claimant's legitimate interests would be compromised by such activity.

11.19.32.   The apparent conflict between *Norbrook* and *Ashcourt Rowan* can be explained by the fact that in both cases the court is applying a fact-sensitive analysis to the protection of the employer's legitimate interests and in particular to confidential information. In *Norbrook*, employment in a different capacity could have led to confidential information being misused, but in *Ashcourt Rowan*, there was a specific finding that the claimant would normally have been alerted to the possibility of confidential information about its clients being misused because clients would have to contact them to obtain release of their files before moving to a new adviser. Hence, the protection provided by the PTR was not justified.

11.19.33.   The third example is *Tradition Financial Services Ltd v Gamberoni* [2017] IRLR 698. The defendant broker challenged the enforceability of the non-competition clause, inter alia on the basis that the capacity in which he could not be employed by the new employer extended to back office work. However, the court found that the confidential information could still be of benefit in back office work. Also, importantly, the validity of the covenant was to be judged on the basis of circumstances at the time it was entered into. The defendant had been engaged in back office work at the point his employment commenced.

11.20.   <u>"Non-poaching" clauses</u>

11.20.1.   In appropriate circumstances, a departing employee can be prevented from poaching or soliciting employees of the ex-employer to join him or her by express covenants justified on the basis of the employer's legitimate interest in maintaining the stability of the workforce.

11.20.2.   Such clauses have been upheld as enforceable where they cover the entire workforce but only in cases relating to small employers (see for example *Hydra plc v Anastasi* [2005] EWHC 1559 (QB), where there were only 12 employees).

11.20.3.   However, normally such clauses need to be limited to employees in a particular team or of a particular level of seniority. If they are too widely drawn there can be a problem showing that a legitimate interest is being protected and there is also the obvious possibility of unwitting breach (see for example *CEF v Mundey* [2012] IRLR 912, where a clause which would have covered a very large workforce was not upheld; the defendant would have known only a very small percentage of them).

11.20.4.   For these reasons, it is desirable for these covenants to be limited to those employees with whom the employee has had some personal contact. This appears to be partly because such restrictions will be more justifiable if they relate to employees over whom the departing employee had some influence and partly because the employer will have a stronger argument if what it is seeking to protect is the integrity of a particular team (see further the references to the 'team' element in non-poaching clauses in *SBJ Stephenson v Mandy* [2000] IRLR 233 and *Dawnay Day v de Braconier d'Alphen* [1998] ICR 1068).

11.20.5.   Where non-poaching clauses are concerned, some similar interpretation issues arise to those found in non-solicitation/non-dealing covenants, such as the meaning of "solicitation" where, in summary, there needs to be an element of persuasion or enticement. An example is *Lomar Global Risks v West* [2011] IRLR 140 where it was found that the departing employee's preparatory discussion of his plans with other employees was not solicitation.

11.21. "Confidential information" clauses

11.21.1. There is an implied duty of confidence in every employment contract. The duty not to disclose the confidential information of the employer also carries on after the end of the employment contract. For this reason, covenants against the disclosure of confidential information are not essential. They can however serve an important purpose in identifying which particular categories of information should be treated as confidential and the kinds of proprietary information for which the employer seeks protection. Identifying that information could also help to support non-competition covenants if it is subsequently contended that one of the reasons for those covenants was to protect confidential information.

11.21.2. In practice, if the employer seeks an injunction to restrain the use of confidential information, it is likely to rely on the implied term and equitable duty of confidence as well as any express contractual covenant.

11.21.3. However, a key point to note is that confidential information clauses will be unenforceable as being in restraint of trade if they purport to prevent the employee from using for the benefit of a new employer information which has become part of his or her general skill, knowledge and experience (see *Ixora Trading Incorporated v Jones* [1990] FSR 251; *Balston v Headline Filters* [1987] FSR 330). If the aim is to prevent the employee providing their knowledge, skill and experience to another employer, or inadvertently using their knowledge of the employer's operation, the courts would expect that to be done by way of a suitable non-competition covenant rather than trying to provide protection against competition "through the backdoor" (per *Reuse Collections v Sendall* [2015] IRLR 226 para 63).

11.22.   Geographical scope of covenants

11.22.1. The question of whether the geographical scope is no wider than is necessary to protect the employer's legitimate interest is usually only relevant to non-competition clauses. There is a close connection between the length of the restriction and the extent of the restraint. If the covenant continues for a long period, a wider area may be harder to justify.

11.22.2. As a general rule, if no area is specified, it will be taken to be worldwide. In modern times, many businesses conduct their business worldwide via the internet or simply by virtue of their global reach. In an appropriate case, a worldwide restriction might be justified and enforceable either on the basis that it is a global market or on the basis that globally, there is only a limited number of competitor organisations which the employee could realistically go to. However, if the reach of the business which the employee has left is limited to certain territories around the globe, a worldwide restriction may not be justified. In *Dyson Technology v Pellerey* [2015] EWHC 3000 (Ch), the claimant sold its products only to 65 countries across the globe. However, the court still upheld a worldwide covenant on the basis that the claimant employer was constantly seeking to expand into new markets around the world.

11.22.3. If the purported basis for the restriction is customer connection, a wide geographical area may be hard to justify because the restriction must correspond with the location of the clientele.

11.22.4. In certain cases, worldwide covenants have been found to be justified to protect confidential information and this is particularly likely to apply to the protection of trade secrets. For example, in the trial of *Poly Lina v Finch* [1995] FSR 751 the Court upheld a worldwide non-competition covenant where the employer stated that the purpose of the covenant was to protect both technical and commercial information. The claimant was a manufacturer of bin liners and the covenant was enforced against their departing marketing director.

11.22.5. There is often a difference in the approach of the courts to rural and urban areas. Wide geographical restrictions may be harder to justify in a densely populated urban area. The classic example is *Office Angels v Rainer-Thomas* [1991] IRLR 214 where the Judge refused to uphold a covenant which prevented recruitment agents working within 1,000 metres of the branch in which they had been employed. The problem was that this market was saturated with hundreds of employment agencies and the radius covered most of the City of London. If the purpose is to protect client connections in an urban area, a restriction accurately based on the post codes where clients reside will be more likely to be effective than one based on a mere geographical radius. A wider restriction may, of course, be easier to justify in a sparsely populated rural area.

11.22.6. Problems can also arise where a geographical limit is defined with insufficient precision. In *Landmark Brickwork Limited v Sutcliffe* [2011] EWHC 1239 (QB), Mr Sutcliffe was the managing director of a specialist brickwork contractor who was summarily dismissed for alleged competitive activity whilst still employed. The covenant prevented him for six months from being employed or engaged in any capacity in any business consisting of or involving distribution or sales of masonry within a "specified area" defined as "Cambridgeshire, Bedfordshire and those parts of the United Kingdom to the south thereof" and "any other place" in which the employer operated its business for the purposes of which Mr Sutcliffe was employed. Slade J held that the geographical scope was too uncertain to be enforceable. No map was appended for "to the south"; "any other place" was too unclear and could mean a town, building, office or building site to which the employer supplied services.

11.22.7.   It follows from the above that the question of what geographic restriction is appropriate depends entirely on the nature of the business and on what legitimate interest the restriction seeks to protect.

11.23.   <u>Duration of covenants</u>

11.23.1.   The longer the duration of the covenant, the less likely it is to be upheld. This is because the covenant must be no wider than is necessary to protect the employer's legitimate interests and also because many covenants prevent the ex-employee from earning a living or impede their ability to do so.

11.23.2.   The question of whether the length is no longer than necessary is fact specific. It is impossible to lay down general rules. However, longer durations are particularly hard to justify for non-competition covenants because they often prevent the employee from earning a living.

11.23.3.   For a recent case where a six-month clause was struck down for being too long, in a non-competition case, see *Monex Europe Limited v Pothecary* [2019] EWHC 1714 (QB) which is analysed in detail above.

11.23.4.   The point is often made that periods of restraint are arbitrary. In *Beckett Investment Management Group Ltd. v. Glynn Hall* [2007] ICR 1539 the Court of Appeal said that the length (in this case the non-competition clause lasted for twelve months) was only arbitrary in the sense that any fixed duration has an element of arbitrariness. The defendant was a financial adviser registered with the FSA, employed by the claimant. His title was "Sales Director". At first instance the Judge had concluded twelve months was too long – he thought three months was enough, rationalising that the claimant needed to approach and attempt to persuade its clients to continue with its services which could be done quickly, and if that failed, the only consequence of the lengthy period was to prevent clients dealing with the people they wanted to deal with. The Court of Appeal disagreed, saying that

a) the Judge's approach was simplistic. The reality was that the defendant and the other ex-employees were highly skilled people and the company would have to recruit and train replacements.

b) The period of twelve months was upheld having regard to the ex-employees' seniority, business patterns, the logistics of replacing them, and industry standard period.

11.23.5. The time required to recruit and rebuild links with clients is often cited to justify the length of restraints. A recent example is *Tradition Financial Services Ltd v Gamberoni* [2017] IRLR 698 where the non-competition clause lasting six months was upheld. The defendant broker had strong personal bonds with clients. It was not unreasonable to contemplate at the outset of the contractual relationship that by the time that relationship came to an end, whenever it did and for whatever reason, the claimant would need a reasonable period in which to shore up its client contacts and to find a replacement to take over from the first defendant in order to protect its legitimate interests. Six months was a reasonable pre-estimate of how long that might take.

11.23.6. The appropriate length of a restraint may depend on the particular industry in two respects. First, some industries have an annual cycle and if there is a legitimate interest in preventing competition, arguably it would make little sense if it lasted for less than 12 months. Examples of such industries are accountancy and the insurance industry, where most policies are renewed annually. Secondly, the courts often have regard to what was the standard length of restraint in the particular industry, presumably because that gives some indication of what is collectively considered to be reasonable and/or necessary.

11.23.7. In deciding what is reasonable, the court may take into account the length of restraints applied to other employees, particularly if they are more senior. In *Taylor Stuart v Croft* (High Court ChD 7.5.97 unreported) a clause prohibiting soliciting clients of the firm for three years was not enforceable for a salaried partner in an accountancy firm. The fact equity partners only had two-year restraints was fatal to the longer period being imposed on a salaried partner. In deciding what would have been reasonable, the Judge said that relevant factors included the fact that the partner knew all the clients in what was a relatively small firm; that in accountancy, a restraint must be for at least a year if it is to be effective at all; and that in the circumstances, two years appeared a reasonable period.

11.23.8. Different rules apply to confidentiality clauses which may be upheld even if there is no limitation of time. In *Mantis Surgical Ltd. v. Tregenza* [2007] All ER (D) 387 Mantis supplied surgical equipment. The defendant, who had held the position of Field Sales Manager for the South of England, resigned and moved to a competitor. Her contract of employment contained a post-termination non-solicitation clause (12 months) and a non-competition clause (3 months). It also included a clause expressly dealing with the use and disclosure of confidential information, but the restriction on use or disclosure was not limited to any particular period, which is not uncommon.

11.23.9. It was accepted by Mantis that an unlimited period of restriction in respect of confidential information was not necessary for its protection. Nevertheless, the Court upheld the clause. The judgment is short but it does encapsulate the reason why confidentiality is treated differently: "...the open-ended nature of the clauses is clearly not as a matter of practicality remotely likely to lead to a life-long ban. It may well be in reality no more than 12 months before the information ceased to be of any relevance or value. The point is that such a time cannot accurately be predicted".

11.24.   <u>At what point in time is the reasonableness of covenants assessed?</u>

11.24.1.   When considering the validity of a covenant, an important point to bear in mind is that the question of whether it is no wider than necessary to protect a legitimate interest of the employer is to be answered with reference to the circumstances when the covenant was entered into, which is often at the beginning of the employment relationship. Subsequent events are not relevant save to the extent they throw light on what might have been fairly contemplated on a reasonable view of the clause's meaning (see for example *Leonard Coppage & Freedom Security Solutions Ltd v Safetynet Security Ltd* [2013] IRLR 970 para 9; *Tradition Financial Services Ltd v Gamberoni* [2017] IRLR 698 at para 47). If the employee has been significantly promoted since then, a point which can legitimately be taken by defendants is that at the relevant time, the employer could not justify such wide covenants.

11.24.2.   On this point, contrast *Bartholemew Agrifoods v Thornton* [2016] IRLR 432, where a covenant was struck down on the basis it had been entered into years previously when the defendant was a trainee, with *Croesus Financial Services Ltd v Bradshaw* [2013] EWHC 3685 (QB), where the defendant was a junior employee, but the fact it was intended that he would be a successor to his father was enough to overcome his junior status.

11.24.3.   An important further point is that while the validity of the non-competition clause has to be judged by reference to the circumstances existing at the date of the contract, the question of whether the employee was acting in breach of the clause has to be judged by reference to when the acts relied on by the employer as constituting breaches took place. So where a restrictive covenant prevented the defendant from being engaged in any activity "which competes with" any trade or business carried on by his former employer, what had to be considered was the relevant areas of competition after termination, not when the employment started: see *Phoenix Partners Group LLP v Asoyag* [2010] IRLR 594.

CHAPTER TWELVE
DAMAGES

12.1.   The context: Remedies in Overview

12.1.1.   Interim remedies, including injunctions, and other non-monetary remedies such as delivery up, have been considered in detail in the previous chapters. A final injunction can also be ordered as a remedy at trial. The courts also have the power to make a declaration.

12.1.2.   The financial remedies available at trial or on summary judgment for a breach of a restrictive covenant and breach of a contractual duty of good faith by an employee are (i) damages or, exceptionally, (ii) an account of profits.

12.1.3.   The same remedies are available at trial for a breach of a duty of confidentiality or breach of fiduciary duty. However, whilst an account of profits is a common remedy for breach of fiduciary duty or breach of the duty of confidence, it is only available for breach of contract where the remedies of damages, specific performance and injunction do not provide an adequate remedy (see *AG v Blake* [2001] 1 AC 268 (HL)). Those circumstances will, in practice, be very rare. Discussion of the process of taking an account for these purposes can be found in other works. The focus of this chapter is damages.

12.2.   Damages based on loss of clients

12.2.1.   Where a claim is based on breaches of implied terms during employment or breaches of restrictive covenants, the normal final remedy will be damages. As a general rule damages will be assessed as compensation for the net loss suffered as a result of the breach of contract, subject to any mitigation by the employer.

12.2.2. The principal damages for breach of a restrictive covenant by the employer will be the loss of net profits caused by the diversion of clients to the defendant. The claimant employer will have to make allowances for costs and expenses he would have had to incur, including a proportion of fixed overheads. It follows that the approach often adopted by claimants in schedules of loss of simply listing the lost turnover in respect of each former client generally does not reflect the true loss. However, if no additional costs would have to have been incurred by the employer to carry out the work for the client, the employer will be entitled to recover the whole fee.

12.2.3. The employer can also claim additional expenses which have been incurred as a result of breach. This is considered below under "Wasted Management Time".

12.2.4. Returning to the lost profits, an attempt will generally be made to quantify the loss caused by the loss of particular clients or the loss of a particular contract or contracts. Sometimes, claimants attempt to do this by listing every client who the competing defendant has dealt with although that may be dependent on obtaining disclosure of this information. When the picture is less clear, an attempt needs to be made to provide the best estimate. Allowance also has to be made for factors such as churn rates, which are a way of assessing what percentage of customers would have been lost in an average year in any event. The other limitation is the fact that once any contractual restrictions had ended, the departing employee would have been able to work with the relevant clients in any event.

12.2.5. Where the claim is based on a departing employee giving a competitive advantage to another business by using improperly removed confidential information or by breaching restrictive covenants, damages can be much more difficult to quantify. One way in which lawyers have recently tried to fill this gap is the use of "Wrotham Park" damages, but recent cases have shown that there are significant limits on the circumstances in which these can be argued for.

12.3. <u>Negotiation or 'Wrotham Park' Damages</u>

12.3.1. 'Wrotham Park' damages are a tool which permits the court to assess damages by reference to what the parties might have agreed for the release of a particular obligation or release of particular information. This originates in *Wrotham Park Estate Co Ltd v Parkside Homes Ltd* [1974] 1 WLR 798, which was not an employment case, but related to the correct measure of damages where a defendant had built on land in breach of property restrictive covenants in favour of the claimant, even though the claimant had suffered no financial loss as a result. The principle was that damages could be calculated by reference to the price which would have been negotiated between the parties for the release of the covenant. This has come to be known as 'negotiation' or 'licence fee' damages.

12.3.2. Consequently, it has been regarded as a remedy which might be available where the claimant has suffered no loss[1] or there would be "difficulty" in establishing loss[2], and it has also been referred to as "exceptional"[3]. The Court of Appeal decision in *One Step (Support) Ltd v Morris-Garner* [2016] EWCA Civ 180 had suggested that such damages might be generally available in a case involving breach of restrictive covenants to provide a flexible remedy when a party could not demonstrate, or had difficulty demonstrating, identifiable financial loss. However, in the same case this approach was rejected by the Supreme Court decision which clarifies that Wrotham Park damages are generally not available for breach of

---

1 As happened on the facts of *Wrotham Park*

2 per *Experience Hendrix v PPX Enterprises* [2003] EWCA Civ 323

3 per *Attorney General v Blake* [2001] 1 AC 268, Lord Nicholls (the "Spy Catcher" case)

restrictive covenants but are, in principle, available for breach of confidentiality (*Morris-Garner v One Step (Support) Ltd* [2018] 2 WLR 1353).

One Step

12.3.3.   In *One Step*, a defendant breached confidentiality whilst still employed by the claimant by sending herself a large volume of documents. On leaving the employment of the claimant, she entered 36-month restrictive covenants and covenants requiring her to keep information concerning its business transactions confidential. However, she set up her own competing company in secret. The non-competition clauses were the crucial part of the settlement agreement that had led to the defendants being paid a large sum of money to sell their shares, and it was found that their breaches of those covenants were deliberate, intended from the very start, and conducted with subterfuge and furtiveness. This last factor meant that *One Step* had been unable to seek an injunction to resolve the dispute at an early stage.

12.3.4.   In the Supreme Court, Lord Reed[4] rejected the proposition that *Wrotham Park* damages are generally available as a type of fall back claim simply because it is a just response. He said that negotiating damages were only available where they reflected the defendant's loss, but in general they would not do so. He said that negotiating damages could only be awarded in the following types of case:

(i)   invasion of rights to tangible movable or immovable property;

(ii) infringement of intellectual property rights;

---

4   who gave the main judgment representing the ratio of the Court's decision; Lady Hale, Lord Wilson and Lord Carnwath agreed; Lord Sumption came to the same conclusion by a different route.

(iii) damages in substitution for an injunction based on the economic value of the right which the court has refused to enforce;

(iv) contract cases but only where the loss suffered is represented by the value of an asset of which the claimant has been deprived such as the right to control the use of land or intellectual property or a confidentiality agreement. Lord Reed rejected the proposition that all contractual rights should be regarded as assets. Certainly the Judge had been wrong in the present case to consider that the claimant had the right to elect how damages should be assessed. The difficulty assessing loss did not justify abandoning the attempt to do so.

12.3.5.   It was only in these cases that the loss can be measured by determining the economic value of the asset in question, because the defendant has taken something for nothing.

12.3.6.   Lord Reed said that where the claimant's interest in the performance of a contract is purely economic, and he cannot establish that any economic loss has resulted from its breach, the normal inference is that he has not suffered any loss. Common law damages were not a matter of discretion and could not be awarded merely to deprive defendants of profits made as a result of the breach, other than in exceptional circumstances.

12.3.7.   Lord Reed acknowledged that the effect of breach of contract in the instant case was to expose the claimant's business to competition which would otherwise have been avoided, but it was not one where it resulted in the loss of a valuable asset created or protected by the right which was infringed. Importantly, Lord Reed acknowledged that the breach of the confidentiality covenant might have been of that character, but in reality the claimant's loss was the breach of obligations of which the non-competition and non-solicitation covenants had been treated as the most significant.

12.3.8. The loss was of profits and possibly goodwill and it was possible to identify that in a conventional manner, even if the loss was difficult to quantify and some elements may be incapable of precise measurement. As a result the Supreme Court ordered a hearing to identify damages by measuring the loss actually sustained. Evidence about a hypothetical release fee was not in itself the measure of the claimant's loss. There was expert evidence measuring the loss of gross profit margin on sales, albeit this was lower than the estimated hypothetical release fee.

Marathon

12.3.9. Prior to the Supreme Court decision in *One Step*, in *Marathon Asset Management v Seddon* [2017] ICR 791 the High Court considered the correct damages in a case where employees had taken confidential information but had not actually used it. Various employees left Marathon, an investment Management Business, and set up a competing business. The employees who left included Mr Seddon and Mr Bridgeman. Mr Bridgeman admitted that over a period of several months before he left Marathon's employment in December 2012, he copied onto USB drives a substantial number of files containing information confidential to Marathon and that he kept these files until the summer of 2013 when they were delivered up to Marathon after proceedings were threatened. He also admitted that, in copying the files and retaining them when he left Marathon, he was in breach of his contract of employment.

12.3.10. Mr Seddon had shared 33 files containing information about Marathon's business with Mr Bridgeman in August 2012 by saving copies on a shared drive on Marathon's computer system. Shortly afterwards Mr Bridgeman downloaded the 33 files to one of his USB drives. The files which Mr Seddon shared with Mr Bridgeman were never used after they left Marathon's employment. Mr Bridgeman made some use of a few of the many other files which he copied but this did not cause Marathon any financial loss or result in any financial gain for the defendants.

12.3.11. Leggatt J rejected Marathon's argument that they should get Wrotham Park damages assessed by valuing all the confidential information in all the documents copied and removed by the defendants on the assumption that the defendants were free to use it. This approach was flawed because of a failure to identify accurately the wrong for which licence fee damages were being sought and to match the remedy to that wrong. It was a fallacy to proceed as if the defendants had purchased the right to use Marathon's files. The following important points emerge from the judgment:

(i) both defendants had breached their implied contractual and common law duties of fidelity to the claimants as well as the confidentiality obligations in their contracts of employment by copying the material; both were jointly liable for breach of confidence founded on a common design in relation to the 33 documents.

(ii) The general object of an award of damages for a civil wrong is to compensate the claimant for injury caused by the defendant's wrongful act. (para 154-155)

(iii) Wrotham Park, or "gain based" damages were an exception, and the mere fact a claimant had not suffered loss did not by itself give a good reason to award gain based damages; (para 212)

(iv) they should only be awarded where compensation was inherently inadequate because it would not represent adequate redress for the wrong done; (para 214)

(v)   the appropriate method of valuation in such a case was to assess the amount of profit made by the defendant that was fairly attributable to its wrongful use of the claimant's property; however, the extent of the misuse of the confidential information had to be identified before valuing its benefit to the defendant, so that the remedy matched the wrong actually committed by the defendant; (para 236 and 265)

(vi) in this case, the claim was based on the wrongful copying of the files and did not extend to their limited use by the defendants – Marathon made it clear they did not advance any case base on the use actually made of the files (para 243); the answer to the question of what a reasonable licence fee would have been to take away confidential information but not use it was nothing (para 283).

(vii) it was irrelevant whether a person who misuses confidential information intends to make wrongful use of more information than he in fact does. That did not affect the damages payable (para 275).

Some conclusions on negotiation damages

12.3.12.   Following *One Step,* if the basis of the claim is loss of clients or loss of profits owing to the defendant's activities in breach of restrictive covenants in a contract, negotiation damages will not be available and attempts will have to be made to value the loss of profit and/or the loss of goodwill from the business. Going forward, a claimant will only be able to have damages assessed on a negotiating basis if an economic value can be placed on the contractual right that is breached, so that it can be considered as an asset.

12.3.13.   If the claim is based on removal of confidential information without permission, in principle damages could be based on valuing the right which created or protected the asset (see

One Step para 95(10)) because the claimant has been deprived of a valuable asset for which it is entitled to require payment.

12.3.14.   The remaining uncertainty is in what circumstances the damages must relate to the use the defendant made of the information and in what circumstances they can be based on a negotiation about the inherent value of the right in the asset, regardless of whether it was used.

12.3.15.   The answer to this in the *Marathon* judgment was that it depends on whether there was a market for the relevant information. If what is taken is a trade secret or confidential business process, the employer would have charged a licence fee for its use which is capable of valuation. But if it is intellectual property which the business would not want to divulge (per *Marathon* para 235) or (by analogy with *Marathon*), business processes, pricing or client information, the court will not value it by reference to an entirely fictional negotiation. In such a case Leggatt J suggests the only way to assess damages is based on the profits actually made via the use of the information. If the information is not used, the notional bargain is for allowing information to be taken of which no use was going to be made, which has no more than a nominal value. However, Marathon is a first instance decision and it was barely referred to in *One Step*.

12.3.16.   In *One Step*, the Supreme Court held that negotiation damages might be available when *"loss suffered was appropriately measured by reference to the economic value of the right that had been breached, considered as an asset where the defendant had taken something for nothing"*. Lord Reed indicates that the only circumstances in which a contractual right can result in loss equivalent to the economic value of the right are a right to control the use of land, intellectual property or a confidentiality agreement.

12.3.17.   Unfortunately, the Supreme Court does not go any further in examining whether such damages might be available for breach of a confidentiality agreement where the information has not been misused and/or the information is not a business process in which the employer would ever wish to sell a licence. It is submitted that if the breach of the confidentiality agreement involved the removal of trade secrets, properly so called, *One Step* might provide a sufficient basis to argue that negotiation damages are appropriate, whether or not the asset was used. It seems unlikely that there are any circumstances where a court would allow negotiation damages to be used as the primary basis for assessing the damages for removal of client information where that had been protected by a confidentiality agreement.

12.3.18.   Lord Reed acknowledged that even in breach of contract cases, negotiation damages still have a role to play in valuing loss. For example, if the parties had been negotiating the release of an obligation prior to its breach, the valuations which the parties had placed on the release fee might be relevant to support, or to undermine, a subsequent quantification of the losses claimed to have resulted from the breach. He also refused to discount the evidential role negotiating damages could play in the present case, in ordering that the trial judge assess damages; however, he did make it clear that the focus was on the actual loss caused by the loss of business, and the expert evidence which went to that question.

12.4.   <u>Other creative damages options</u>

(i)   repayment of salary

12.4.1.   Various attempts have been made by employers to reclaim salary which was paid by them to employees at the time the employees were allegedly breaching their duty of fidelity or fiduciary duty. There have also been attempts to claim salary paid to the employees by a competitor after they have departed. Shortly stated, the position is that it might be possible in principle to reclaim salary but there seems to be no reported case in which the attempt to do so has been successful.

12.4.2.   In *Gamatronic (UK) Ltd v Hamilton & Mansfield* [2017] BCC 670 (the facts of which are set out above) the employer's claim for repayment of salary was based both on the breach of fiduciary duty as an equitable remedy, and breach of contract. The court held that the fiduciary could be made to repay fees received if s/he was in breach of duty. However, fees would not be repaid if the fiduciary had continued to be a valuable and diligent employee. The two defendants had not been dishonest for much of the relevant period and had spent only a fraction of their time on the rival business. As to breach of contract, the money was claimed on the basis that they had not devoted their full time and attention to the business.

12.4.3.   It was found they had spent only a fraction of their time on the new business, had continued diligently with their duties for the employer and brought in a substantial proportion of its turnover. Mr Hamilton was by far the most successful salesperson in the business, responsible for about two thirds of the turnover. Ms Mansfield meanwhile attended to the day to day management needs of the business and stayed for three months after she had given up her shares to deal with handover issues. The evidence did not establish that they had failed to devote proper time and attention to their work. There was no evidence that their activities had actually given them any head start. In the circumstances, the claims for repayment of salary failed.

12.4.4.   The court said there was no authority for awarding damages in such a situation, but in any event, there was no breach of the contractual provision. The employer had the benefit of the valuable work for the period in question.

12.4.5.   The employer also claimed compensation equivalent to salaries they had received working at the competitor, on the basis that a fiduciary in breach must account for his profits. The court said whilst this was correct in principle, the profits claimed must bear some relationship to the breach of duty. There was a gap of at least nine months between the breaches of duty and the earning of the salaries claimed. Hence there was no reasonable relationship between the claim and the breach of duty.

12.4.6.   A similar claim was made in *Brandeaux Advisers v Chadwick* [2010] EWHC 3241 (Ch). The company provided investment advice. The dismissed employee had transferred large amounts of confidential material to her home email in order to arm herself in the event that a future dispute with her employers arose. She had compliance responsibilities and was also concerned that she may need to protect her position with the regulators. At trial it was found that her actions were a repudiatory breach of contract. The employer sought to reclaim salary paid to her after the point she started breaching confidentiality. It was argued that from that point on she was in breach of contract and in breach of her fiduciary duty for not informing them of what she was doing. The High Court rejected this claim as the employer could not show the company suffered any loss. She had been working as usual and the employer had taken the benefit of that work.

    (ii)   Wasted management time

12.4.7.   Another damages option which employers are frequently unaware of is a claim for wasted management time. Where a departing employee has caused difficulty (for example trying to poach clients who have to be won back and damage to business property and systems which have to be rectified) it is important to consider all the losses which flow from that breach.

12.4.8. The claimant employer is entitled to claim for the additional damages he has incurred as a result of the breach, such as the costs of recruiting new sales staff where others have left. Some other examples from the case law where such damages have been claimed are:

> (i) *Flogas Britain Ltd v Calor Gas Ltd* [2013] EWCH 3060 (Ch): costs associated with staff visiting existing customers to stop them changing to a new supplier;

> (ii) *R & V Verischerung AG v Risk Assurance & Reinsurance Solutions SA* [2006] EWCH 17005 (Comm): the costs of investigating a conspiracy between employees.

12.4.9. This gives rise to the question of how these losses might be quantified. One basis is on an hourly rate basis in respect of work done by the staff. This is supported by clear authority in cases involving the need to put matters right following the negligence of IT contractors and can be relied on even in the absence of contemporaneous records: see *Tate & Lyle v. GLC* [1982] 1 WLR 149.

12.4.10. In *Horace Holman v. Sherwood International* [2001] (QB), LTL 14/11/2001, Judge Bowsher QC said:

> "…in principle a claimant may be able to claim for the expense of time lost by directors and staff, although there may be difficulties of proof where time has not been recorded. In *Tate & Lyle v. GLC* [1982] 1 WLR 149…Forbes J. indicated that in principle, there should be compensation for the cost of managerial time wasted. He also found that in that case there was no evidence that managerial time has been so spent…I cannot and do not say, in the absence of records there is to be no recovery." (paras 72-73)

12.4.11.   There was also a successful claim for damages based on wasted management time in *Bridge UK v Abbey Pinford* [2007] EWHC 728 (TCC), where the wasted time was caused by the defendant's negligent installation of a printing press. Whilst remedial works were required, the claimant had to outsource its printing to a third party, whilst continuing to pay wages. The wasted executive time was that of Mr Ruck the business director. His assessment of loss was based on a retrospective assessment of the time he had spent dealing with the problems connected with the installation. The Judge awarded a proportion of his annual salary, discounted by 20% to reflect the inherent uncertainties of this approach.

AFTERWORD

As stated in the Preface, the author's intention is to provide a 'quick reference' guide and an explanation of the things which matter most. The question of how the law is likely to develop is beyond the scope of this book and will be left for other works. Where the cases leave questions unanswered, an attempt has been made to make clear in the text the areas where the law has room for further development. It is however sobering to reflect on the fact that when *Egon Zehnder Ltd v Tillman* came to the Supreme Court in 2019, it was over a hundred years since the highest court in the land had addressed the interpretation of restrictive covenants. Given that most aspects of the wider law of Employee Competition are derived from the common law rather than statute, the progress of significant development is unlikely to move at speed.

INDEX

MORE BOOKS BY
LAW BRIEF PUBLISHING

A selection of our other titles available now:-

'Covid-19, Homeworking and the Law – The Essential Guide to Employment and GDPR Issues' by Forbes Solicitors
'Covid-19, Force Majeure and Frustration of Contracts – The Essential Guide' by Keith Markham
'Covid-19 and Criminal Law – The Essential Guide' by Ramya Nagesh
'Covid-19 and Family Law in England and Wales – The Essential Guide' by Safda Mahmood
'Covid-19 and the Implications for Planning Law – The Essential Guide' by Bob Mc Geady & Meyric Lewis
'Covid-19, Residential Property, Equity Release and Enfranchisement – The Essential Guide' by Paul Sams and Louise Uphill
'Covid-19, Brexit and the Law of Commercial Leases – The Essential Guide' by Mark Shelton
'Covid-19 and the Law Relating to Food in the UK and Republic of Ireland – The Essential Guide' by Ian Thomas
'A Practical Guide to the General Data Protection Regulation (GDPR) – 2nd Edition' by Keith Markham
'Ellis on Credit Hire – Sixth Edition' by Aidan Ellis & Tim Kevan
'A Practical Guide to Working with Litigants in Person and McKenzie Friends in Family Cases' by Stuart Barlow
'Protecting Unregistered Brands: A Practical Guide to the Law of Passing Off' by Lorna Brazell
'A Practical Guide to Secondary Liability and Joint Enterprise Post-Jogee' by Joanne Cecil & James Mehigan

'A Practical Guide to Chronic Pain Claims' by Pankaj Madan
'A Practical Guide to Claims Arising from Fatal Accidents' by James Patience
'A Practical Guide to Subtle Brain Injury Claims' by Pankaj Madan

These books and more are available to order online direct from the publisher at www.lawbriefpublishing.com, where you can also read free sample chapters. For any queries, contact us on 0844 587 2383 or mail@lawbriefpublishing.com.

Our books are also usually in stock at www.amazon.co.uk with free next day delivery for Prime members, and at good legal bookshops such as Wildy & Sons.

We are regularly launching new books in our series of practical day-to-day practitioners' guides. Visit our website and join our free newsletter to be kept informed and to receive special offers, free chapters, etc.

You can also follow us on Twitter at www.twitter.com/lawbriefpub.

Printed in Great Britain
by Amazon